BY THE WAY . . .

Authors: Laurie Evans Frantz, Lesley S. King, Marti Niman

Editors: Emily Drabanski, Penny Landay, Walter K. Lopez

Design and Production: Bette Brodsky

Map Conversions and Illustrations: Bette Brodsky

Library of Congress PCN Number: 2001012345

ISBN: 978-1-934480-07-6

Printed in China

BY THE WAY . . .

25 A GUIDE TO NEW MEXICO'S SCENIC BYWAYS

CONTENTS...

* National Scenic Byways

INTRODUCTION . . .

By the way . . . New Mexico has 25 Scenic Byways and they all have a story to tell!

I invite you to use this book as a guide to discovery as you travel New Mexico's Scenic Byways. Marti Niman and I have written a series of stories that are designed to give the reader an overview of some of the many scenic and cultural destinations along the byways.

Travel writer and photographer Lesley S. King shares essays and photos from her personal experiences on the byways in the sections titled "Roadside Attractions." I encourage you to climb into the car with a good friend, throw this book on the dashboard, take off and create your own adventures. The fold-out map in the back flap will help you chart your course.

New Mexico's 25 Scenic Byways offer a passport to adventure. They lead to big-sky ranchlands, mountains redolent with ponderosa pine, spectacular archaeological ruins and undulating sand dunes. New Mexico's Scenic Byways stimulate economic development, particularly tourist destinations in rural New Mexico. They showcase places that many people, New Mexicans and out-of-state visitors alike, may not discover otherwise.

Scenic Byways are designated based on at least one of six intrinsic

qualities: cultural, historic, archaeological, recreational, natural and scenic. Most of New Mexico's Scenic Byways can claim all six of these qualities. Eight of our byways are recognized with national designations, more than any other state except Colorado and Oregon. National designation indicates that the byway has regional significance.

The National Scenic Byways Program, a grass-roots collaborative effort, was established in 1991 to help recognize, preserve and enhance selected roads throughout the United States. The vision of the program is to create a distinctive collection of American roads and to showcase their stories and treasured destinations. Byway communities strive to create wonderful travel experiences and enhance the quality of local life by preserving, protecting, interpreting and promoting the intrinsic qualities of byways.

Travel our byways to places you've dreamed of but never expected to find.

—Laurie Evans Frantz
New Mexico Scenic Byways Program Manager

J-9 NARROW GAUGE RAILWAY ...

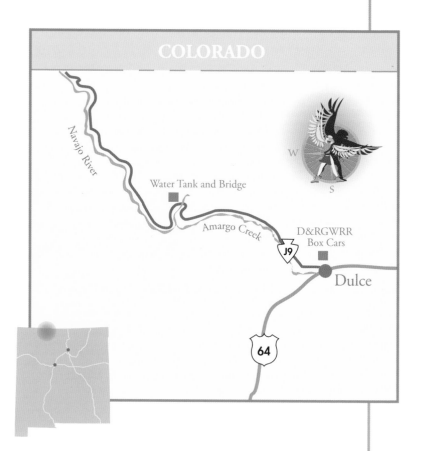

COLORADO

Navajo River

Water Tank and Bridge

Amargo Creek

D&RGWRR
Box Cars

J9

Dulce

64

The J-9 Narrow Gauge Scenic Railway Byway has had many twists and turns, both literally and historically. This isolated road winds through a beautiful and dramatic landscape.

The byway started as a primitive trail forged by early settlers and miners, and became a crude toll road in 1877. The Denver and Rio Grande Western Railroad laid track on the same alignment in the late 1800s. It has come full circle—the track has been removed and it is once again a largely unimproved road, now known as Jicarilla 9.

The Denver and Rio Grande Railway Company, incorporated in 1870, planned to lay track from Denver to El Paso, Texas, and ultimately to Mexico City. Six branches would serve the booming silver mining areas of Colorado. Both the rough terrain and the cheaper cost of construction and operations led to the company's decision to use narrow gauge track, with rails laid 3 feet apart rather than the standard 4 feet 8.5 inches. Minimal grading was done in preparation for laying the track, and the line ran through narrow canyons and over steep grades.

In late 1881, the San Juan branch was completed from Antonito to Durango, Colorado, and from there to Farmington and Chama connecting the east and west sides of the Rocky Mountains. It served isolated farming and mining areas, transporting raw materials like timber and mineral ore, passengers and tourists. After the silver boom ended in 1893, the freight shifted to agricultural products and timber milled by a Pagosa Springs, Colorado, lumber company. By 1915, the timber supply had nearly disappeared, and the company moved its operations to Dulce, a station on the San Juan branch, where it built a new mill and company town in 1916.

The Cumbres & Toltec Scenic Railroad, a narrow-gauge steam engine running between Chama and Antonito, Colorado, remains a popular tourist attraction.

Photo courtesy N.M. Tourism Department

In 1935 the San Juan branch stopped operation for freight shipment completely, in 1951 it discontinued daily passenger service and in 1968 it was abandoned between Chama and Durango. The Cumbres-Toltec and Durango-Silverton lines, which continue in operation today as tourist lines, are all that remain of the San Juan branch. It doesn't take a railroad buff to enjoy the sound of a steam engine and the rhythmic clack of wheels on the narrow gauge, and the mountain scenery is enchanting.

The greatest significance of this corridor today is that it connects the sovereign nations of the Jicarilla Apache in New Mexico and the Southern Ute in Colorado. J-9 facilitates the exchange of commodities and religious and cultural heritage between the two tribes.

The Utes are the oldest continuous residents of Colorado. Two of the seven original Ute bands, the Mouache and Capote, make up the present-day Southern Ute Indian Tribe. They reside on approximately 800,000 acres in southern Colorado. The Jicarilla Apache Tribe consists of two bands: the Llaneros, or plains people, and the Olleros, or mountain valley people. They once roamed a large part of northeastern New Mexico and southern Colorado.

In 1887, the Jicarilla Apaches were given a permanent reservation in north-central New Mexico, which now encompasses 1 million acres. J-9 parallels or overlays about 10 miles of the old railroad bed from Dulce northeast to the Colorado border. Most of the original track has been removed, but a short segment remains at the junction of U.S. 64 and J-9 (called Narrow Gauge Street here) in Dulce. Two old Denver and Rio Grande Western Railroad wooden boxcars sit next to the Jicarilla Culture Center. Several yellow frame buildings with rust trim along the road in town were obviously associated with the railroad, but they have second careers as tribal administration buildings.

The canyon closes in on the paved road as it continues northwest alongside Amargo Creek. After about four miles, the pavement and the creek disappear. The Navajo station stop was here at the confluence of Amargo Creek and the Navajo River. Still present to testify to the presence of busier times are a round, yellow water tank with rust-red roof and timber supports and a steel-truss bridge across the river. A plaque on the bridge states that this was once the Denver and Rio Grande Western Railroad Royal Gorge Route Scenic Line. Where tracks once were, planks were laid to allow cars over the bridge. It outlived even that use and has now been bypassed completely by a modern concrete bridge to the west. Fortunately, it has been allowed to remain, an elegant witness of earlier times.

Continuing north, the road narrows, and rock outcrops and tall pines loom down from either side. Horses graze by the river, which at this time of year is iced over completely in some places.

Where you can see it, black water races to Colorado. This is not a road to drive in wet or very cold weather. Where it isn't snow-packed, it is deeply rutted by previous travelers who may or may not have had the luck (like I did) to have been rescued by one of the eight Game and Fish officers who patrol the reservation's one million acres.

Riding in a train through these narrow, winding canyons must have been an adventure in the late 1800s. Traveling this road is still an adventure, even in the comfort of an automobile.

The Cumbres & Toltec Scenic Railroad offers rides out of Chama, not far from the J-9 Narrow Gauge Railway Scenic Byway.

Photo by Steve Larese

—Laurie Evans Frantz

Weaving Beauty

O ften in life I'm called upon to adapt to new circumstances, whether I like them or not. From lemons, I make lemonade. On a recent trip en route to the J-9 Narrow Gauge Railway Scenic Byway, I get to see this principle in action. I drive into Dulce, the Jicarilla Apache Nation headquarters, a cluster of houses in a bowl-like valley framed by pine-covered hills. Black storm clouds billow above, the sun occasionally slanting through a hole.

The weather casts a mercurial air over the village that may just reflect the history of these Athapascan people. Proud nomads, for centuries they roamed broadly across northern New Mexico, southern Colorado, Kansas, Oklahoma, Texas and Nebraska. In 1887, they settled on this 1,364-square-mile reservation. It's a stunning place of high desert and rolling mountains, but it called on them to stay in one place.

At the center of town, I step into the Jicarilla Apache Arts and Crafts Shop and Museum, on U.S. 64, where I get a sense of the resilient way these Apaches have made a life for themselves here. Under luminescent lights, a band of women work and talk, and on this special day, sell cookies and chocolate cake.

I start by exploring their modest museum. Cases line the walls, filled with moccasins, dolls in elaborately beaded dresses, drums, fire-scarred micaceous pottery and, most notably, baskets. Jicarilla, the name given this tribe by the Spaniards, derives from the word *jícara,* meaning "small cup," one item the Apaches often wove with reeds. Today, their art has expanded far beyond utilitarian vessels to lovely works that could only be called art.

Rowena Mora, a shy woman with smooth skin and dimples on her cheeks, points out some of her baskets in the museum case. A

3-foot-wide piece has a rainbow of colors radiating outward. "As you go along you start weaving a design," she says of her process. "And as you keep going, it just comes, but I try to stay with the traditional ideas." By that she means patterns such as stars and diamonds.

Returning to the worktable, I watch the women weave baskets from sumac—a reed they pick along the Navajo River. Some of them string beads as well. Generations of Jicarillas have spent their time here in this way. Today, the sound of country music twangs from a radio, occasionally a voice speaking Jicarilla Apache inter-rupting to make local announcements. With a bag of oatmeal cook-ies in hand I head out, inspired to weave, from the sumac of my life—beauty.

Rowena Mora displays her basket woven from the sumac she collects along the Navajo River.

Opposite, inset: Fly-fishing
Photo by Steve Larese

WILD RIVERS BACK COUNTRY ...

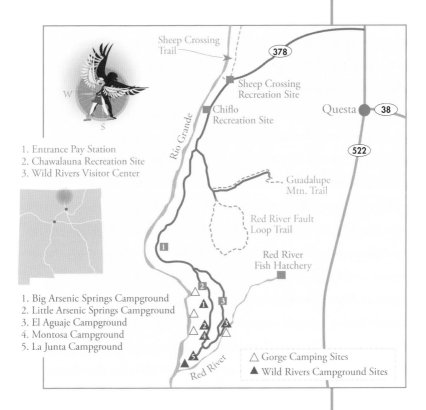

Sheep Crossing Trail

378

Sheep Crossing Recreation Site

Chiflo Recreation Site

Questa

38

Rio Grande

522

W

S

1. Entrance Pay Station
2. Chawalauna Recreation Site
3. Wild Rivers Visitor Center

Guadalupe Mtn. Trail

Red River Fault Loop Trail

Red River Fish Hatchery

1. Big Arsenic Springs Campground
2. Little Arsenic Springs Campground
3. El Aguaje Campground
4. Montosa Campground
5. La Junta Campground

△ Gorge Camping Sites
▲ Wild Rivers Campground Sites

Red River

*Petroglyphs on rocks along Big Arsenic Springs Trail
in the Wild Rivers Recreation Area offer a reminder
of those who walked this path centuries ago.*

Photo by Dan Monaghan, N.M. Tourism Department

The sagebrush and piñon-juniper flatlands of the Taos Plateau are sliced by a steep chasm of black rock carved 600-800 vertical feet to a ribbon of river, circled by volcanic cones, cliffs and the Sangre de Cristo's white-dusted peaks.

Deceptively tame, the Wild Rivers Back Country Byway provides ready access to the rock-strewn, riffling upper reaches of the Río Grande before dams and diversions dampen the river's unruly ways–a haven for hikers, cyclists, wildlife-viewers, sport-fishermen and sightseers. The spectacular 360-degree vista at La Junta Overlook, where the Red River joins the Río Grande 800 feet below, is singularly worth the drive.

The byway loops through the Wild Rivers Recreation Area, man-aged by the Bureau of Land Management Taos Field Office and is open year round, although it may be snow-packed in winter. Beginning about two miles north of Questa on N.M. 378, the road winds between Our Lady of Guadalupe Church and the flag-studded cemetery in the agricultural village of Cerro. As the byway enters the pungent sage flats, Cerro Chiflo is visible jutting out of the gorge at Bear Crossing. On clear days, the frothy peaks surrounding Mount Blanca in Colorado peek over the horizon's edge. Dirt parking areas dot the road at trailheads bearing such colorful names as Chawalauna, El Aguaje and Big and Little Arsenic Springs.

Rumor has it that Big Arsenic Springs were so-named because a her-mit living at the bottom of the gorge told folks there was arsenic in the water so he could keep it to himself. Today, Big Arsenic Springs offers a self-guided nature trail, a developed campground and trail access to the river, where visitors may hear the cascading song of a canyon wren or the whistle of a hawk overhead. Several trails reach the river and backcountry campsites at the bottom of the gorge. Porous volcanic rocks tumble down the cliffs into the water, useful as stepping-stones or basking boulders for those in a lizard state of mind.

Guadalupe Mountain, Red River Fault and Rinconada hiking and biking trails explore the diverse geology and plant life of the Taos Plateau, ranging from the level stroll of Rinconada loop's wide gravel path along the rim to the 1,000-foot uphill grunt at Guadalupe Mountain, which rewards the energetic with expansive views, tall pines, wildflowers and cool air. La Junta Trail descends sharply in a series of switchbacks, stairs and a ladder to the Red River-Río Grande confluence, where ponderosa pines offer tall shade for trout anglers.

The Taos Plateau is the largest volcanic field within the Río Grande Rift, its layers of thick basalt deeply sliced north-south by the river. Rifts are cracks in the earth's crust along faults that pull apart, tilting downward to form a valley and mountains. Here, the Sangre de Cristo Range edges the horizon to the east and the Tusas Mountains to the west, while numerous dormant volcanic cones pop impertinently out of the broad tortilla flatlands of sage. Ute Mountain looms to the north and the domes of Pot Mountain and San Antonio Peak to the west and northwest—all three providing habitat to elk, mule deer and pronghorn as well as coyote, badger and other wildlife.

A fly-fisherman enjoys an after-noon casting his line into the Río Grande.

Photo by Mike Stauffer, N.M. Tourism Department

Below, left*: Some of the state's best rafting can be found in the upper stretch of the Río Grande.*

Photo by Steve Larese

Red-tailed hawks circle the cliffs and mesas, their tails flashing copper in the sunlight, while mountain bluebirds dart across the mesa like tiny pieces of the Southwestern sky torn off and set aflight. Mule deer drift soundlessly at dusk and tracks of cougar and bear may be traced in the sand.

The upper reaches of the Río Grande offer a whitewater wonderland for kayakers and rafters in years of abundant snowfall. The river enters New Mexico like a lamb and then, at the Class 4 Razorblade Rapids near Ute Mountain, it begins to roar like a lion. Dropping 200 feet per mile into the Upper Taos Box, it is too dangerous for rafting until it reaches the mellower flows at the Río Grande-Red River confluence. Boating within the Wild Rivers Recreation Area is hazardous and requires a permit, while swimming is dangerous due to swift currents and icy temperatures.

Anglers find the challenge of rainbow trout, northern pike and brown trout enhanced by deep pools and a rush of rapids that echo from black cliffs framing a sliver of sky. Those feisty browns grow up from small fry that "trek" the steep icy trails each winter, packed in 5-gallon water jugs on the backs of Game and Fish officers and volunteers from the Bureau of Land Management, the Carson National Forest and local sportsmen's groups. The annual Río Grande Brown Trout Trek is a midwinter work party shared by local fishing enthusiasts and biologists. Nearby Red River State Fish Hatchery raises trout for stocking the gorge and other waters in the area. Fishing licenses and a habitat stamp are required and may be purchased in Questa.

The byway loops past the Wild Rivers Visitor Center, open daily from Memorial Day to Labor Day, which contains a mural painted by a collaboration of New Mexico artists who share a passion for the area and its wildlife. Most visitors to the area find its rugged yet accessible wildness engenders a passion of its own.

—Marti Niman

Opposite: A llama takes a drink at Big Arsenic Springs on the Río Grande.
Photo by Lesley S. King

A Passion for the Great River

I 've had a long-standing love affair with the Río Grande. As a whitewater kayaker, I've spent decades floating serenely through its canyons and getting pummeled in its rapids. I've paddled sections near the Colorado border, including the Taos Box, south of there in Pilar, farther south through Española, and even in Albuquerque. Today, however, I get to experience the great river in another way.

I cruise along the Wild Rivers Back Country Byway through miles of sage forest cut by the 800-foot-deep Río Grande Gorge.

Soon I get my first glimpse of the dramatic and foreboding canyon that always inspires me with awe. This gorge, unlike Arizona's Grand Canyon, which is made mostly of sandstone, is cut through iron-hard black basalt, a true miracle of nature.

I meet my guide for the day, who has brought along llamas to carry our little band of hikers' gear down into the canyon. My llama, a white male named Zeus, sings hello to me with a harmonica-like hum. Once we've secured our lunches in the llamas' packs, we descend into the canyon. The views from the Big Arsenic Trail encompass long stretches of the gorge, with glimpses of the turquoise-green Río Grande below. Holding a rope, I lead Zeus, who steps agilely behind me.

After more than an hour of hiking, we reach the river—my love—and I rush to be on its shores. Right here it is nestled deep in the canyon, so very few people get to experience it. It is truly a wilderness, with massive boulders dotting the shore and wildlife such as rabbits and squirrels darting through the trees. We even pass a lion's den, imprinted with tracks.

Converging with the river, Big Arsenic Springs offers an enchanting blue pool, where Zeus and the other llamas bend their necks down to drink. While sitting on the grassy shore, we eat a lunch of salami and provolone on sourdough bread, with sprigs of spicy watercress harvested from the spring.

On our way back, we find graceful petroglyphs that depict deer, bighorn sheep, eagles and spiral-symbols that tell the story of the Ancestral Puebloans' journeys. They, too, lived with—and loved—this Río Grande.

Right: An ancient petroglyph of a bighorn sheep or deer.
Photo by Lesley S. King

Opposite, inset: Río Grande Gorge Bridge.
Photo by Steve Larese

Opposite, below: Taos Pueblo

ENCHANTED CIRCLE . . .

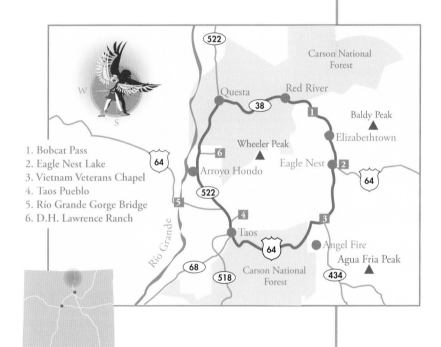

1. Bobcat Pass
2. Eagle Nest Lake
3. Vietnam Veterans Chapel
4. Taos Pueblo
5. Río Grande Gorge Bridge
6. D.H. Lawrence Ranch

522

Carson National Forest

Questa

Red River

38

Baldy Peak

1

Elizabethtown

Wheeler Peak

6

64

Arroyo Hondo

Eagle Nest

2

64

522

5

4

Taos

3

64

Angel Fire

Río Grande

Agua Fria Peak

68

518

Carson National Forest

434

Taos Pueblo is a designated UNESCO World Heritage Site.

Photo by Mike Stauffer, N.M. Tourism Department

The Enchanted Circle Scenic Byway offers a taste of everything that's New Mexico. It links the oldest, continuously occupied residence in New Mexico, Taos Pueblo, with Angel Fire, which was incorporated in 1986.

The Enchanted Circle is home to the United States' first memorial to Vietnam War veterans. It passes by Elizabethtown, New Mexico's first incorporated town, now a ghost town. Much of the byway traverses land formerly part of the Maxwell Land Grant, once the largest private, individual holding in the Western Hemisphere. The movie industry discovered this area long ago, producing such films as *Butch Cassidy and the Sundance Kid* and *Easy Rider*.

The byway begins in Taos, on N.M. 522. The first to call the Taos Valley home were Tiwa-speaking Pueblo Indians, who settled there about 1,000 years ago and built two communal dwellings on either side of Río Pueblo de Taos. Taos Pueblo's beautiful multistory skyline was already there when Hernan de Alvarado arrived in 1540. The upper stories can only be reached by ladders, since there are no interior stairways. Modern utilities are prohibited in this part of the pueblo.

Taos was established about 1615 as an outpost of New Spain. It was an early gathering place for mountain men, including Kit Carson and Ceran St. Vrain. Taos has been an artists' haven ever since the Taos Society of Artists was formed in 1914. Later, art patron Mabel Dodge Luhan brought noted artists, photographers and authors such as D.H. Lawrence, Georgia O'Keeffe, Nicolai Fechin and Ansel Adams. The town provides a treasure trove of old homes, museums, interesting shops and art galleries.

The Río Grande Gorge Bridge, 12 miles northwest of Taos on U.S. 64, is a must-see side trip. When the structure was built in the mid-1960s, it was called the "bridge to nowhere," because funding didn't exist to continue the road on the other side. The Río Grande Gorge Bridge is the second-highest suspension bridge in the United States.

Returning to the Enchanted Circle, Arroyo Hondo is nine miles north of Taos on N.M. 522. It grew out of an 1815 Spanish land grant on the Río Hondo. In the 1960s it was the home of the New Buffalo commune. Hippies from the commune have since dispersed into the general population of northern New Mexico, adding their own flavor to the local culture.

The entrance to the D.H. Lawrence Ranch is on the way to Questa. Lawrence only spent 11 months in New Mexico, but it influenced him profoundly. He wrote parts of several works here, and his ashes are housed in the ranch's memorial chapel. The ranch is now owned by the University of New Mexico, which uses it for educational, cultural and recreational purposes.

The next stop is Questa. Settled before the 1840s, it is situated in the middle of wonderful hiking trails and campgrounds, including those at Cabresto Lake, Mallette Canyon and Midnight Meadows.

East on N.M. 38 from Questa and traveling toward Red River, the road offers a roller coaster ride. Red River was settled by miners from Elizabethtown in the late 1800s. The mines eventually closed, and the town is now known for its beautiful, high-alpine scenery, skiing, fishing and switchback roads through old mining country.

Opposite: The chapel at the Vietnam Veterans Memorial State Park, near Angel Fire.

Photo by Dan Monaghan, N.M. Tourism Department

The road runs through Bobcat Pass at 9,820 feet and descends into the high-alpine Moreno Valley. The valley is bounded by some of the most spectacular peaks in New Mexico: Agua Fria at the south end, Baldy on the north and Wheeler on the northwest. Wheeler Peak, at 13,161 feet, is the highest point in New Mexico.

Captain William Moore and friends successfully panned for gold in the Moreno Valley in the mid-1800s. Word leaked out, and Elizabethtown was born as a tent city in the 1860s. By 1871, mining operations had virtually shut down, and a fire in 1903 left the town to the ghosts. The shell of the stone Mutz Hotel guards the meager remains of E-town.

N.M. 38 ends at Eagle Nest, nestled in the Moreno Valley. A tiny jewel of a lake adorns the village. Eagle Nest Lake, owned by the state, is stocked with kokanee salmon, and rainbow and cutthroat trout. The nomadic Mouache Utes called the glow caused by the sunset on Agua Fria Peak the "fire of the spirits." Franciscan friars later changed this to "fire of angels." Angel Fire was named after the old legend. The byway continues to Angel Fire on U.S. 64.

The chapel at the Vietnam Veterans Memorial State Park is a soaring white structure pointing to the sky from a hill just west of Angel Fire. Inside the simple monument are photographs of Vietnam casualties and a shrine of mementos and candles left by visitors.

The Enchanted Circle closes in Taos, entering town on tree-lined Kit Carson Road. What more could a traveler ask than a road that ends at its beginning and offers such wonders in a day's drive?

—Laurie Evans Frantz

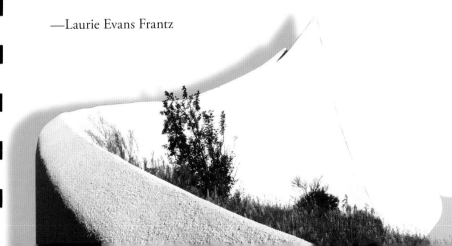

Northern New Mexico's Playground

Ever since I was a young girl, the Enchanted Circle has been my playground. My family owned a cabin at Taos Ski Valley, so we spent most winter weekends and holidays racing over the slopes of one of the premier skiing and snowboarding destinations in the West. Its 72 trails are mostly challenging, but the Kachina Bowl offers skiing for intermediates, and the renowned ski school can help anyone enjoy the sport.

In summer months, Taos offered my family plenty of excitement as well. We used to hike four miles to fish for trout and camp at Williams Lake above Taos Ski Valley. When I grew old enough, I took my first hike to the craggy summit of the state's tallest peak, 13,161 Wheeler, a full-day or overnight adventure with views in every direction.

The rest of the Enchanted Circle offers rich adventure as well. A resort popular with Texans, the Red River Ski and Snowboard Area has 58 mostly gentle runs and offers fun features for families such as their Moon Star Mining Camp, with easy trails, a replica 1890s mine and a log cabin. After skiing all day, I've spent many a winter night in the town of Red River, when it takes on a honky-tonk flavor, with live country music playing in the local bar and thick cuts of beef being grilled in the steakhouse.

As I've grown older, I've come to enjoy a more peaceful kind of skiing—cross-country. Some of the state's best is farther around the Enchanted Circle at the Enchanted Forest Cross Country Ski and Snowshoe Area. I enjoy kicking and gliding along its 18 miles of groomed trails that traverse pine and aspen forests, and stopping for spectacular views out across the broad Moreno Valley.

The last big adventure spot on the Enchanted Circle is Angel Fire. My first snowmobiling ride took place at the Angel Fire Resort, where I cruised through the pristine alpine forest. Through the years, I've enjoyed skiing the 73 trails there, which range broadly, so any ability level can be satisfied.

But my most memorable experience of Angel Fire took place on horseback. We rode high into the mountains, stayed the night at a cow-camp cabin and finished by herding cattle along Eagle Nest Lake. At the end of the day, we tied up our horses at a hitching post and had a beer in Eagle Nest's historic bar. A variety of rides are available from Angel Fire—all one needs is a sense of adventure.

Cowboys herd cattle in the Enchanted Circle.

JEMEZ MOUNTAIN TRAIL . . .

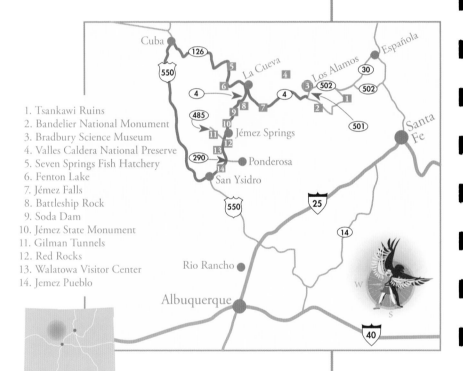

1. Tsankawi Ruins
2. Bandelier National Monument
3. Bradbury Science Museum
4. Valles Caldera National Preserve
5. Seven Springs Fish Hatchery
6. Fenton Lake
7. Jémez Falls
8. Battleship Rock
9. Soda Dam
10. Jémez State Monument
11. Gilman Tunnels
12. Red Rocks
13. Walatowa Visitor Center
14. Jemez Pueblo

Cuba

Española

La Cueva

Los Alamos

Jémez Springs

Santa Fe

Ponderosa

San Ysidro

Rio Rancho

Albuquerque

The Jémez Mountain Trail twists through time and terrain, contrasting vermilion desert cliffs and snowy alpine peaks, 13th-century stone dwellings and the birth of the Atomic Age in nearly the same breath.

Travelers may fish canyon waters at dawn, explore ancient Pueblo ruins, don snowshoes for a woodland trek and view elk crossing an immense volcanic caldera—all in the same day.

The trail begins at the junction of U.S. 550 and N.M. 4 in the pastoral village of San Ysidro, named for the patron saint of farmers. Passing a restored church of the same name, N.M. 4 slowly winds past Jemez Pueblo, home to more than 3,000 tribal members who call the village "Walatowa" in their native Towa language. Jemez Pueblo sits at the gateway to the spectacular Cañón de San Diego, where the road bisects reddish-orange cliffs as it enters the Jémez Mountains. The Walatowa Visitor Center is wedged in these rocks, along with roadside stands selling crafts, fry bread, and red and green chile stew. Jointly operated by Jemez Pueblo and the Santa Fe National Forest, the visitor center houses a museum and gift shop and provides information about the area.

A side trip three miles east on N.M. 290 offers a winery tour, several artisan galleries and an RV park. Past the red rock cliffs, another side trip on narrow N.M. 485 leads to the Gilman Tunnels, blasted through rock during the 1920s for logging trains passing along the Guadalupe River Gorge.

At N.M. 4 and N.M. 485, Virgin Mesa towers above the junction of the Jémez and Guadalupe rivers. The

Opposite, inset: Battleship Rock, a few miles north of Jémez Springs.

Photo courtesy of N.M. Tourism Department

canyon narrows as N.M. 4 passes several developed picnic and fishing access areas and campgrounds along the Jémez River, part of the Jémez National Recreation Area.

N.M. 4 cuts through quaint Jémez Springs, dwarfed by high volcanic cliffs that echo the rushing waters of the Jémez River. The village has numerous restaurants, B and Bs, galleries, a country store and a saloon resplendent with swinging doors, a stone fireplace and antlers from every ilk of wild critter found in these parts. Weary travelers may wash the dust off with a dip in the past at the Jémez Springs Bath House, built between 1870 and 1878 and now run by the village. The natural hot spring is enclosed by a well structure built in the 1920s as a WPA project, and is so rich in minerals it must be drilled out on occasion.

Jémez State Monument protects the stone ruins of Giusewa, one of numerous villages built 600 years ago in the canyon and on mesa tops by the Jemez people, who numbered around 30,000 at the time of contact with the Spanish *conquistadores* in 1541. The Spaniards established a Roman Catholic mission at Giusewa and the massive stone walls of San José de los Jémez were built about the same time the pilgrims landed at Plymouth Rock. The church ruins sit beside those of Giusewa, meaning "place of the boiling waters" in Towa.

Boiling waters steam up the canyon at Soda Dam—an unusual formation of colorful "petrified" water shaped like a domed waterfall, where the Jémez River bubbles into the hot springs rising along a deep fault. A few miles north, Battleship Rock rises sharply from the riverbed like a lost ghost ship run aground while cone-shaped tent rocks poke out from opposite cliffs. A few miles north, a short, steep climb to Spence Hot Springs rewards hikers with a choice of hot and warm pools and sweeping views of the canyon below.

Scenic vistas await visitors at the Valles Caldera National Preserve.

Photo by Mike Stauffer, N.M. Tourism Department

At La Cueva, travelers may continue east on N.M. 4 to Los Alamos or turn northwest on N.M. 126 to Cuba. N.M. 4 loops through the Santa Fe National Forest, a rolling woodland of spruce and fir dotted with campgrounds and trailheads for access to hiking, fishing and snow sports. One short trail leads to Jémez Falls, where the river drops 70 feet in a series of waterfalls. Adventurous hikers may hop the trail spur to McCauley Warm Springs for a backcountry soak.

The 89,000-acre Valles Caldera National Preserve contains one of the largest, young volcanic calderas in the world—now a breathtaking

Hiking trails at Bandelier National Monument provide a bird's-eye view of the Ancestral Pueblo ruins.

Photo by James Orr

expanse of mountain meadow and forest. The preserve offers premium fishing, hunting, hiking, wildlife viewing and snow sports by advance reservation.

N.M. 4 descends sharply in a series of switchbacks to meet N.M. 501, a detour into a futurist world of science at Los Alamos National Laboratory (LANL). One of the major scientific institutions in the world, LANL's core mission is national security. Although closed to the public, LANL operates the Bradbury Science Museum to provide a peek into the recent past of Robert Oppenheimer's life and the Manhattan Project as well as current, cutting-edge technologies.

For a peek into the remote past, continue east on N.M. 4 to Bandelier National Monument, housing several thousand Ancestral Pueblo dwellings within almost 33,000 acres of steep-walled canyons, mesas and wilderness. Just past the town of White Rock, a short trail leads to the "sky-city" ruin of Tsankawi, perched atop a cliff-ringed island mesa.

Returning to La Cueva and heading west on N.M. 126 Fenton Lake State Park offers fishing, camping, cross-country skiing and ice fishing on a 35-acre lake beneath tall ponderosas. N.M. 126 curves north past Seven Springs Hatchery, remodeled as a breeding facility for Río Grande cutthroat trout. Rainbow trout are stocked in a pond open only to anglers 12 and under and over 65. The road winds through the Santa Fe National Forest to the town of Cuba, gateway to the 41,000-acre San Pedro Parks Wilderness and Chaco Culture National Historical Park. At the intersection of N.M. 126 and U.S. 550, the Cuba Regional Visitors Center features arts and crafts and provides area information. Heading south on U.S. 550, watch for the volcanic plug called Cabezón Peak, rising 2,000 feet from the valley floor and thought to be the head of a creature slain by Monster Slayer in Navajo stories. U.S. 550 soon crosses the starting point at San Ysidro as the terrain gradually flattens, gently returning travelers to I-25 and the 21st century.

—Marti Niman

Note: N.M. 126 is unpaved between mile marker 33 and mile marker 13.5 and is closed for winter from late January until the beginning of March.

Sensual Delight

When I was a teenager, "the Jémez" was synonymous with a kind of hippie decadence. Everyone knew that was where peopled bathed in forest hot springs—*naked*.

It doesn't surprise me that the area drew lovers of sensuality. When I travel along the Jémez Mountain Trail National Scenic Byway today, I count on a sensual feast.

I'll start with a wine tasting in Ponderosa, one of the oldest wine-making regions in the United States, where I savor a slightly sweet Riesling, with an aroma of apples. Next, I stop along N.M. 4 to sample some Indian fry bread, which during the warm months members of Jemez Pueblo cook along the roadside. I'll smother the crispy wafer with honey and eat it using both hands, the sweet nectar inevitably sliding down my forearms.

By the time I reach Jémez Springs, I'm ready for a soak at one of the bath houses—and a massage, too, on days when I'm feeling extravagant. The warm water, rich in minerals, tingles across my skin, leaving me so blissed out I have to sit down for lunch. Much of the fare here heralds back to the days when the hippies used to pervade the place. Cute little cafes with brightly painted walls serve black-bean burritos and homemade apple pie.

The next leg is pure visual pastry as I pass by the Soda Dam, with its blue-ice-like structure, and the regal Battleship Rock, which seems to float in the forest. I stop to gaze across the broad bowl of the Valles Caldera National Preserve, imagining it erupting nearly a million years ago, when it spread ash as far away as what are now Kansas and Nebraska.

Opposite: Marlene Gachupin cooks frybread during the Pueblo Independence Day Celebration in the village of Giusewa.

Saving Los Alamos and Bandelier for another trip, I make my way through the mountains past the pine-surrounded Fenton Lake and over to Cuba. In that town of some 600 residents, high on the Continental Divide, still another feast awaits—some of the state's best New Mexican food at El Bruno's Restaurante y Cantina, where I savor a combination plate with lots of *picante* red chile. On my way home, I gaze at the noble flat-topped 7,785-foot Cabezón Peak, my senses sated and happy.

PUYE CLIFFS . . .

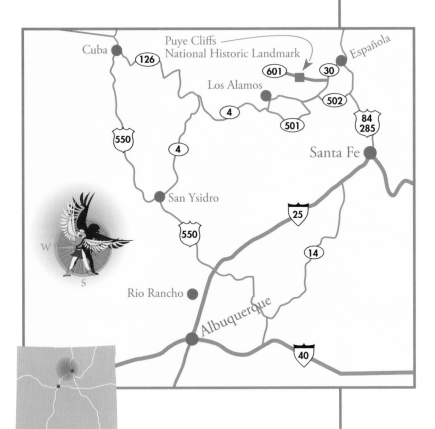

Cuba

126

Puye Cliffs
National Historic Landmark

Española

601

30

Los Alamos

502

4

501

84
285

550

4

Santa Fe

San Ysidro

25

550

14

Rio Rancho

W

S

Albuquerque

40

Puye Cliffs Scenic Byway is a pleasant drive through four of New Mexico's seven life zones, an area of low hills blanketed by piñon, juniper and grama grass.

Its seven short miles give no indication of the spectacular surprise that awaits a traveler at its termination—the towering heights of Puye Cliff Dwellings, a National Historic Landmark.

Puye Cliffs is the ancestral home of the present inhabitants of Santa Clara Pueblo, one of New Mexico's 19 pueblos. More than a thousand people reside in the pueblo. Their native language is Tewa, which they share with Nambe, Pojoaque, San Ildefonso, Ohkay Owingeh and Tesuque pueblos. In Tewa, Santa Clara Pueblo is called Kha'p'oo Owinge, "valley of the wild roses." Puye translates as "where the rabbits gather."

The rolling hills start to flatten out after a few miles of driving, and the road continues to climb. Puye Cliffs is visible in the distance, and the Jémez Mountains appear on the horizon. Piñon-juniper gives way to ponderosa pine at the base of the mesa on which the Puye Cliffs are carved. The portion of the road open to the public ends at the cliff dwellings. No one lives on Indian Service Route 601 (the official designation for the byway), but tribal members still do some dry farming beyond the cliff dwellings.

As you pull in to park for your tour of the ruins, you will see a view very similar to the one that visitors saw in the early part of the 20th century. Two buildings stand at the base of the mesa, both made from shaped volcanic tuff blocks found at the site. The building on the left

Opposite, inset: Ruins at Puye Cliffs National Historic Landmark.

Photo courtesy of Santa Clara Pueblo

is now an interpretive center, and the building on the right is a gift shop. Together they originally constituted a Harvey House, the only one built on an Indian reservation. In the 1920s, Fred Harvey made an agreement with the tribe: Tourists staying in Harvey House hotels in Las Vegas, Lamy or Santa Fe could sign up for his Indian Detours to Puye and Santa Clara Pueblo to purchase pottery. His guests traveled via the "Chili Line," the narrow-gauge Denver and Rio Grande Western Railroad. Built in the late 1870s, it connected Española with Antonito, Colorado. From Santa Clara, guests were driven to Puye in a covered wagon, and in later years a Model T.

Santa Clara now offers tours of Puye Cliffs led by native members of the community. Looking up from the paved path at the interpretive center, you will see dwellings the length of the cliff face. Holes and eroded tuff blocks are all that remain of two levels of rooms. Handholds and toe holes cut into the rock of the cliff face connect the two levels of cave dwellings. Prehistoric paths lead to the top of the mesa. Nowadays ladders assist climbers in their journey from the cliff face to the ruins of a mesa-top village. If climbing ladders on cliff faces makes you dizzy, you can drive to the top. The elevation there is 7,200 feet, about 400 feet higher than at the interpretive center.

The mesa-top pueblo is the largest ancestral native settlement on the Pajarito Plateau. Puye Cliffs supported a population of 1,500 people from the 900s to the late 1500s. The inhabitants farmed on the fertile bench above the creek that flows south of the mesa.

Opposite and above: Santa Clara Pueblo tribal members give tours of the Puye Cliff Dwellings.

Photos courtesy of Santa Clara Pueblo

Drought forced them to move to their present home in the Río Grande Valley in 1580.

Puye was excavated by Edgar Hewett in cooperation with the Southwest Society of the Archaeological Institute of America in 1907. The tribe restored six structures between the cliff dwellings and the pueblo through a summer youth project in summer 2009. Santa Clara worked closely with Bandelier National Monument to use authentic construction materials.

Be sure to visit the present-day pueblo, which is 10 miles east of

Puye. It is famous for its handcrafted, polished black-and-red pottery, but its many artists also produce jewelry, baskets, paintings and other distinctive works of art. Santa Clara has four events that are generally open to the public: Kings' Day (January 6), St. Anthony's Feast Day (June 13), Santa Clara Feast Day (August 12) and Christmas Day dances (December 25).

The Puye Cliffs Scenic Byway was closed after the Cerro Grande fire of May 2000. The fire burned 48,000 acres in the Los Alamos area and reached as far as Garcia Canyon, just south of Puye. A large area of vegetation was bulldozed to keep flames from jumping to the ruins. The fire's destruction of trees that held topsoil in place caused sediment to flow into Santa Clara's four lakes, which affected the drainage around the byway and the stability of the road. The road has now been repaved and the culverts replaced, and it is safe for travelers again.

To visit Puye Cliffs, head southwest from Española on N.M. 30. Five miles south of the city you will see the Puye Cliffs Welcome Center, where you must pick up your tickets for one of the guided tours. Look above the counter, and you'll see a preview—a beautiful photomural of the cliff dwellings displayed on the wall. Guided tours are by a tribal member. Admission fees and departure times vary for the different tours. Call ahead for group reservations. A full-length tour into prehistory lasts approximately two and a half hours and includes the cliff face and the mesa-top settlement.

—Laurie Evans Frantz

Opposite: Nancy Youngblood of Santa Clara Pueblo and one of her exquisite pieces of pottery.

Photos courtesy of Nancy Youngblood

From Ancient to Now

On a recent trip along the Puye Cliffs Scenic Byway, I get to see the way a Native people have sustained their culture for hundreds of years. I meet a guide at the base of the famed Puye Cliffs National Historic Landmark. An older Santa Claran, he leads our little group up to some 740 rooms carved into chalky volcanic tuff and then onto the mesa top, where a maze of ruins spreads out across the prairie.

As we walk, he tells of the Santa Claran traditions, pointing to potsherds from ancient vessels lying in the sand. They remind me of a visit I had to Santa Clara Pueblo a number of years ago, when I wrote about Nancy Youngblood, who still makes pottery the way her ancestors did. She invited me up into the hills to dig for rosy-brown clay, which we brought to her home. There she showed me how to

strain and knead it to make the pots for which she and generations of her family—the Tafoyas—are so renowned.

Next, under a metal basket in her studio, she stacked wood and lit it into a blaze. Into the flames she placed her delicate melon bowl. It's a work reminiscent of her ancestors' pottery, but this, in a brilliant swirl, catapults the vessel to a new level. At the end of the firing, she adds horse manure to create a dramatic black color. "The fire decides the pot's destiny," she said. Most of her works have ambitious futures. They sell to people all over the world and have garnered awards ranging from Best of Class at the Gallup Inter-Tribal Indian Ceremonial to Best of Show at the Santa Fe Indian Market.

Once I leave the ruins of Puye, I make my way to the old Santa Clara village, 10 miles to the northeast. It is a cluster of modest adobe homes surrounding their 1918 church. Whenever I come here, I always peek over the cemetery wall to see the enchanting tangle of crosses and headstones. Then I wander through the shops, where artists sell their own crafts—jewelry and paintings but, most importantly, the Santa Claran incised red pots and black pots that are a testament to a people's determination to not only preserve culture but also to evolve it.

Opposite, inset: A hiker explores a trail in the Santa Fe National Forest.

Opposite: Golden leaves shimmer at Aspen Vista, a popular hiking trail in the Santa Fe National Forest.

Photos courtesy of N.M. State Parks

SANTA FE NATIONAL FOREST . . .

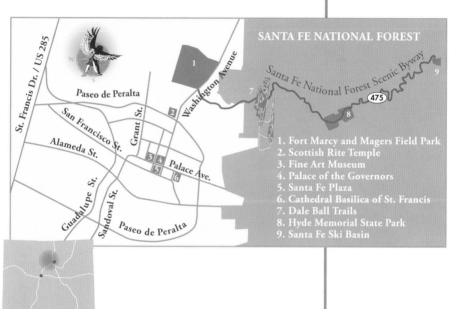

SANTA FE NATIONAL FOREST

Santa Fe National Forest Scenic Byway

475

1. Fort Marcy and Magers Field Park
2. Scottish Rite Temple
3. Fine Art Museum
4. Palace of the Governors
5. Santa Fe Plaza
6. Cathedral Basilica of St. Francis
7. Dale Ball Trails
8. Hyde Memorial State Park
9. Santa Fe Ski Basin

St. Francis Dr. / US 285
Paseo de Peralta
San Francisco St.
Grant St.
Washington Avenue
Alameda St.
Palace Ave.
Guadalupe St.
Sandoval St.
Paseo de Peralta

Where else can one shop for handmade Native American crafts under the shady portal of a 17th-century Spanish adobe capitol in the morning and trek into a 12,000-foot alpine wilderness that afternoon?

The Santa Fe National Forest Scenic Byway originates near downtown Santa Fe, not far from the oldest public building in America—the Palace of the Governors—and loops 15 miles through an aspen-evergreen forest to Ski Santa Fe. En route, vast vistas of amber-tinged badlands, azure mountains and abundant opportunities to hike, bike, ski, camp, picnic or snowshoe make this byway a refreshing break from Santa Fe's cultural deluge.

Several blocks north of the Santa Fe Plaza, at the intersection of Washington Avenue and Paseo de Peralta, the byway originates near the immense lipstick-pink Scottish Rite Masonic Temple, built in 1911 and modeled after the Moorish architecture of the Alhambra, in Spain. The building's Pepto Bismol stucco coat is a blazing color digression from the regulation adobe brown of Santa Fe's historic center. Open to the public, it is rumored that Elvis might live here—or occasionally haunts its hallways.

At the Artist Road turnoff, city-run Fort Marcy Complex offers recreational facilities and hosts the annual Burning of Zozobra, the kick-off to the Santa Fe Fiesta in early September. One of the Kiwanis Club's less staid fundraisers, Zozobra is a 50-foot animated marionette representing bogeyman Old Man Gloom. It is set on fire to banish the community's woes and troubles while the crowd chants, "Burn him, burn him!" As one reveler said, "It's a rare chance to get really crazy—legally."

Left: Towering aspens brighten the way along Hyde Park Road.

Photo by James Orr

The original Fort Marcy was built by the U.S. Army in 1846, marking the U.S. acquisition of New Mexico in the Mexican-American War.

Artist Road winds through several residential neighborhoods and accesses the northern portion of the Dale Ball Trails, a 30-mile system of loops through the piñon-juniper foothills for hikers, runners and mountain bikers. Artist Road becomes N.M. 475 and enters the Santa Fe National Forest, a cool haven from the desert sun with its ponderosa, spruce, fir and white-barked, gold-leaved aspen trees. The road jogs through Hyde Memorial State Park, where the massive stone-and-log Hyde Park Lodge recalls fabled Old World hunting castles. Built by the Civilian Conservation Corps in 1938, it served as a Girl Scout retreat and the original Ski Basin Lodge. The 350-acre park was named for naturalist and businessman Bennie Hyde, whose widow donated the property in 1938 as one of New Mexico's first state parks. For campers who prefer the comfort of civilized digs, the park offers seven electric sites in addition to group shelters, picnic areas, trails and 50 developed campsites.

Re-entering the Santa Fe National Forest, the byway horseshoes 3,353 vertical feet through several climatic life zones and ends at the ski basin. Trailheads, picnic areas and camp-grounds beckon travelers into the back-country, where aspen meadows and sparkling waterfalls could lead one to forget this is the high desert—if not for the vistas of the Arroyo Seco badlands beyond.

Opposite: The Hyde Park Lodge once was the original Ski Basin Lodge.

Photo by Mike Stauffer, N.M. Tourism Department

At the ski basin, a wooden bridge connects to the Winsor Trail—a short and sweet grunt uphill that lands the intrepid hiker at the gateway to the spectacular 223,333-acre Pecos Wilderness—land of bighorn sheep, black bear, elk and native Río Grande cutthroat trout.

Winter snowfall lures snowshoers and cross-country skiers to back-wood trails and downhill skiers and snowboarders to the groomed slopes of Ski Santa Fe, where chairlifts rise 1,650 vertical feet to Tesuque Peak at 12,000-feet elevation. Here the view encompasses 7,000 to 11,000 square miles and backcountry adventurers often schuss through the trees to the neighboring Aspen Vista Trail, where they hitch a ride back to the easy lift uphill.

The lifts are not limited to winter months only. When the aspen leaves burst into fiery gold and crimson in late September, the chairs offer a relaxing trip upslope through woodlands that seem to be at finger's reach. In autumn, the hillsides take on an almost ethereal, shimmering aura when angled sunlight filters through the quaking leaves.

Visitors may retrace the same route downhill to return to Santa Fe and chase away their own bogeymen at a Japanese-style spa on the way—if the retreat into the rarified air of the forest byway hasn't already worked its magic.

—Marti Niman

Opposite: Snow drapes the mountains throughout the winter in the Santa Fe National Forest.

Photo by James Orr

Circling through Time

O n rock faces throughout the Southwest, Native Americans have carved petroglyphs in the form of spirals, which symbolize their intricate spiritual journey. The symbols remind me of the circular nature of life, the way experiences keep coming around until we learn the lessons from them. My trip near the Santa Fe National Forest Scenic Byway starts at the New Mexico History Museum, which takes me on such a spiral journey.

The *Telling New Mexico* exhibit starts in a round room reminiscent of a Pueblo place of worship called a kiva, adorned with pottery, basketry and beadwork, and highlighted by birds chirping and Native Americans telling stories. I get a sense of the early days of the region, where tribes lived in harmony with nature.

As befits this storyline, the museum circles me into the next phase of history. I come upon the many changes the Spanish brought starting in the 16th century. Their armor, weaponry and household utensils show how they created from their old life in Spain a new one here, while a painted *retablo* illustrates the ardor of their Catholicism.

That established lifestyle was altered as well, with the coming of the Santa Fe Trail in 1821, when merchants, trappers and mountain men arrived. Their story comes alive before me, as vivid recordings from travel journals play. With the help of artifacts and electronic media, wars in the region spark to life as well: the Mexican/ American, the Civil War, and smaller battles in Lincoln and Colfax counties. I even find spurs of the notorious outlaw Billy the Kid.

Continuing on my spiral, a train toot introduces the next big influx of change—the railroad, which arrived in the late 1800s. Artists came soon after, their presence celebrated here with an

Tourists and vendors under the portal at the Palace of the Governors in Santa Fe.

enlarged photograph of Taos painter Ernest L. Blumenschein. Another historic shift brought scientists from around the world to Los Alamos to work on the Manhattan Project. A film of the first atomic bomb explosion in 1945 marks that shift.

I finish my tour in front of the Palace of the Governors, back to the start with the Native Americans. As I peruse their jewelry and other crafts, a vendor with long black braids framing her face smiles at me. I smile back, aware of the spiraling nature of history, which has brought each new influx of change, and a sense that from it, we just might be kinder.

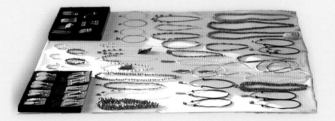

SANTA FE TRAIL . . .

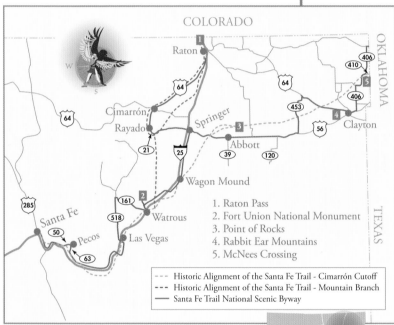

COLORADO

OKLAHOMA

Raton — **1**

64 — 64 — **406** / 410 — **5**

Cimarrón — 64 — 453 — 406 — **4**

Rayado — Springer — **3** — 56 — Clayton

21 — 25 — Abbott — 39 — 120

Wagon Mound

285 — 161 — **2**

Santa Fe — 518 — Watrous

50 — Pecos — Las Vegas

63

TEXAS

1. Raton Pass
2. Fort Union National Monument
3. Point of Rocks
4. Rabbit Ear Mountains
5. McNees Crossing

- - - Historic Alignment of the Santa Fe Trail - Cimarrón Cutoff
- - - Historic Alignment of the Santa Fe Trail - Mountain Branch
——— Santa Fe Trail National Scenic Byway

The year was 1821. It seemed the only way to satisfy his debts, so William Becknell placed an advertisement in the newspaper asking for a "company of men" to trade "to the westward."

In September of that year, they left Franklin, Missouri. Transporting their goods on pack animals down old trails used by Indians and frontiersmen, they reached Santa Fe, Republic of Mexico, which had only recently gained its independence from Spain. They entered present-day New Mexico through Raton Pass. Thus was forged the Mountain Branch of the Santa Fe Trail.

Crossing Raton Pass was the hardest part of traveling the Mountain Branch. Richens "Uncle Dick" Wootton established a toll road through the pass in 1865, charging $1.50 for wagons, 25 cents for horses, and five cents a head for stock; Indians used the road for free. Interstate 25 parallels the old road. The byway follows Moulton Street southeast to Second Street in Raton, first known as Willow Springs. It became a water stop for stagecoaches and a freight stop on the Santa Fe Trail.

The byway picks up south of Raton on U.S. 64 and runs through Cimarrón. Settled around 1844, it became the headquarters of the 1,750,000-million-acre Maxwell Land Grant in 1857. Wagon trains entered the plaza from the east after crossing the Cimarrón River. Lucien Maxwell built the Aztec Mill, which survives as the Old Mill Museum (open summers). The St. James Hotel started as a saloon in 1872 and was expanded in

Opposite, inset above: Native American artists sell their work under the portal at the Palace of the Governors on Santa Fe's Plaza.

Photo by Dan Monaghan

Opposite, below: Intricately designed pots are sold at the Santa Fe Indian Market.

Photo by Steve Larese

1880. First floor rooms are named for the cowboys and outlaws who stayed there—people such as Bat Masterson, Buffalo Bill Cody and Jesse James.

Heading south, the byway passes through Rayado, a campsite on the Santa Fe Trail and a strategic point where the Mountain Branch intersected two other trails. In 1849, Lucien Maxwell and Kit Carson decided to settle there and build a fort to safeguard travelers. A federal garrison post was established there in 1850.

In 1822, after the huge success of his first trip, Becknell and 22 men loaded three prairie schooners with goods for a second expedition. Wagons couldn't cross the mountains, however, so this time they headed south across the prairie from Cimarrón, Kansas. Entering New Mexico north of present-day Clayton, they created the Cimarrón Cutoff. North of Clayton, N.M. 406 intersects McNees Crossing, where the trail forded the North Canadian River.

The byway travels west out of Clayton on U.S. 56 past Rabbit Ear Mountains, an important landmark on the trail. Point of Rocks, another significant trail land formation, is north of U.S. 56 about 22 miles east of Springer. The party of Santa Fe merchant J. W. White was attacked near here in 1849, and 11 graves are at the site. Now a private ranch, Point of Rocks Ranch is open to the public. Call for more information and directions.

Springer, located six miles west of where the Trail crossed the Canadian River, is home to the Santa Fe Trail Museum housed in the 1882 Colfax County Courthouse.

The byway leaves Springer on the east I-25 frontage road and heads for Wagon Mound, the last major landmark on the trail, named for its resemblance to the top of a covered wagon.

The Mountain Branch and the Cimarrón Cutoff intersected at Watrous, and then the trail went west to Fort Union. Visitors can

Pecos National Historical Park preserves 12,000 years of history, including that of the ancient Pecos Pueblo and a Spanish Colonial mission.

Photo by James Orr

learn more about this important military post at Fort Union National Monument. The first of three forts was built here in 1851 to protect Santa Fe Trail travelers and supply other New Mexico forts. The melted adobe walls of the last fort stand on a rise, commanding an unobstructed, 360-degree view of the prairie.

Las Vegas was founded in 1835, and it became a major trading center on the trail. The byway follows the I-25 frontage roads east and then N.M. 63 into Pecos. Pecos Pueblo was still inhabited when the Santa Fe Trail opened in 1821, but after it was abandoned in 1838 it was used as a campsite by Santa Fe Trail travelers. Kozlowski's Ranch

was a trading stop and stage station on the trail. Both of these historic stops on the Santa Fe Trail are part of Pecos National Historical Park.

A granite marker on the Santa Fe Plaza commemorates the physical end of the trail. But the arrival of the railroad in Santa Fe in 1880 marked the literal end of almost 60 years of caravans rolling into the old town. Now trains transport freight through the mountains and across the prairie. The wagons may be gone, but the spirit of the Santa Fe Trail still lives.

—Laurie Evans Frantz

Fort Union National Monument showcases the remains of an important military outpost that was built to protect travelers on the Santa Fe Trail.

Opposite: A granite obelisk in the center of the Santa Fe Plaza marks the end of the Santa Fe Trail.

Photos by Steve Larese

Historic Trail Offers a Warm Welcome

I grew up in the 1850s Watrous House that was once a stage-coach stop along the Santa Fe Trail. As was the custom of such haciendas, it was a large quadrangle, built around a courtyard, with gates on two sides so that wagons could drive in and be locked away from the many dangers of these broad plains.

Even though the trading days at our hacienda were long gone, the Watrous House continued throughout my youth to serve as a stopping point for travelers along I-25. These ranged from family friends to curious strangers, who would timidly knock at the front door of the big white house and ask if it was a museum or hotel. My mother would often invite them in to sip coffee and eat fresh-baked sour-dough bread.

I relate this story because, though the wagons ceased traveling the Santa Fe Trail more than a century ago, it still welcomes travelers into the doors along its route, whether at stopping points such as our home or others that are open to the public.

Some of my favorite stops include the Raton Historic District, on the town's First and Second streets. There I peruse antique shops, art galleries and an enchanting Mission-style train station that sells regional art. South of there I stop at the Old West town of Cimarrón. The 1872 St. James Hotel hosted the likes of Wyatt Earp, Jesse James and Annie Oakley. Today, it offers good food and a frontier style that encourages lounging. The town's main street welcomes visitors with a few galleries, artist studios and shops selling souvenirs and espresso.

I really tend to linger at the Las Vegas Plaza, once a trade center on the Trail, where mercantile pioneers Charles Ilfeld and Don Benigno Romero prospered. I'll have lunch at the 1882 Plaza Hotel,

Galleries and colorful shops line the streets in Cimarrón.

and then stroll around the historic district, with its lush elm trees, galleries, antique stores and bookshops.

My journey culminates at the Trail's terminus, the Santa Fe Plaza. I shop for Native American jewelry under the portal of the Palace of the Governors and sit on a bench to eat ice cream. Sometimes I'll strike up a conversation with others enjoying the welcoming arms of the Trail.

HISTORIC ROUTE 66 . . .

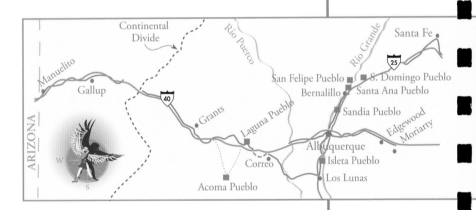

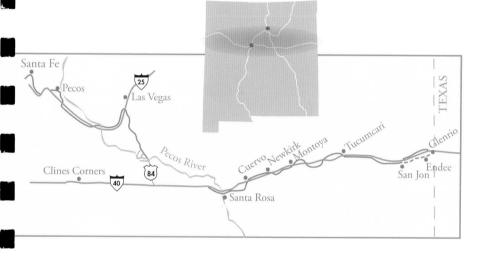

Santa Fe

Pecos

25

Las Vegas

TEXAS

Clines Corners

Pecos River

Cuervo Newkirk Montoya Tucumcari

Glenrio

84

40

San Jon

Endee

Santa Rosa

The legendary Route 66 Scenic Byway enters New Mexico
from Texas across a vast, sunlit prairie and crisscrosses
I-40 in a ribbon of time, dropping in and out among
warp-speed semis and SUVs into a two-lane highway
that meanders through rocky outcrops, quiet streams and
adobe villages.

Parts of the byway disappear beneath cow pastures or the interstate,
and the effect is startling—an instantaneous shift from the manic present to a not-so-distant time at once hip and innocent. Along the way,
the high-desert landscape is both austere and sublime, its red-hued cliffs
dropping off into immense *llanos*, or pine-wooded hills and valleys.

Tucumcari Mountain is the first harbinger of high country to come
as it pokes up off the plains southwest of its namesake town, gathering
clouds from across the prairie around its blunt-shaped peak. Motels
and 1950s diners with restored neon signs line Route 66 through the
center of town. Santa Rosa, to the east, straddles the Pecos River in
an oasis of artesian lakes, its Blue Hole plunging 240 feet beneath the
stark desert floor and luring scuba divers from across water-challenged
New Mexico. Santa Rosa's airport tarmac covers a portion of the earliest Route 66, and old billboards painted on boulders south of town
still peddle their wares to passing travelers. A railroad bridge featured
in John Ford's 1940s film, *The Grapes of Wrath*, now transports trains
across the Pecos River.

Route 66 dead-ends just east of town and travelers are thrust back on
I-40 to U.S. 84 north, which re-emerges as old Route 66 at Dilia and
meets I-25 to the north at Romeroville. Here the byway winds westward
through the wooded foothills of the Sangre de Cristo Mountains among
villages, where the communities center their spiritual and physical heart

The colorful neon lights of the Blue Swallow Motel in Tucumcari add to the allure of Route 66.

Photo by Steve Larese

around adobe churches that predate Route 66 by roughly a century. Near the village of Pecos, Pecos National Historical Park houses a huge complex of ancient Pueblo ruins and two Franciscan missions dating from the 17th and 18th centuries. Among Santa Fe's adobe and stucco buildings are several structures that housed a series of businesses since the 1930s—mere newbies by Santa Fe's millennial origins.

The original Route 66 descended La Bajada's 6-percent grade in a series of hairpin, hair-raising switchbacks in a 500-foot, 1.4-mile descent toward Bernalillo. If the road was unchanged today enterprising folks surely would produce bumper stickers and T-shirts proclaiming, "I survived La Bajada." As it is, today's travelers can be grateful for the streamlined descent on I-25, from which they can pick up the byway for a leisurely drive through pastoral Algodones and into bustling Bernalillo. Here, Route 66 follows the original El

One of the highlights of the Gallup Inter-Tribal Indian Ceremonial is the festive parade.

Photo by Steve Larese

Camino Real, which linked the Spanish colonies 400 years ago.

Old Town, in Albuquerque, shelters the 1706 vintage church San Felipe de Neri and preserves the Spanish Colonial ambience in its narrow *caminos*, which curve gracefully among shops and courtyards.

Albuquerque is a four-way crossroads of Route 66 in New Mexico, where a turn in any direction leads up the old highway and its quirky scattered remnants. Heading east on Central Avenue offers some of the best-preserved motel courts, diners and theaters before the road cuts through Tijeras Canyon between the Sandía and Manzano mountains into Moriarty and Edgewood. Recently painted stencils along old Route 66 in Moriarty are prototypes for painting the entire route across New Mexico—an effort to identify the byway despite vintage nostalgia collectors' propensity for lifting old Route 66 signs. Heading south from

Albuquerque to Los Lunas, the byway sidesteps Isleta Pueblo before it veers west to Correo and the Parker Pony Truss Bridge, near I-40.

Travelers may opt to stay on a rough section of the byway or briefly jump on I-40 to Mesita, where the byway slices through some spectacular red-rock cliffs past Dead Man's Curve and Turtle Rock. Laguna Pueblo perches on a hilltop where travelers may glimpse the white-washed San José de la Laguna Mission Church of 1699, nestled among the still-older village *casitas*. The Sky City of Acoma has been inhabited since 1150 atop a 357-foot-high mesa, its spectacular views overlooking a green valley circled by cliffs and mesas. The Sky City Cultural Center includes the Haak'u Museum, which offers an extensive collection of art and artifacts, as well as educational programs on one of the oldest still-intact civilizations of North America. The uranium boomtown of Grants sits astride Route 66 and its classic assortment of neon signs, motor courts, cafés and theaters along the main street.

Continuing westward, old trading posts and gas stations dot the byway as it passes crimson sandstone cliffs into Gallup, "Gateway to Indian Country" and host of the Gallup Inter-Tribal Indian Ceremonial. Part powwow, part rodeo, beauty pageant and parade, the Gallup Inter-Tribal Indian Ceremonial celebrates Native American cultures across the Southwest and beyond.

Travelers who opt for the Mother Road of Route 66 in New Mexico are advised to arm themselves with maps and road guides before setting out. The many twists, turns and dead-ends of Route 66 among modern highways can leave even the most well-oriented travelers slightly dazzled by more than heat and high elevation. In this case, the journey is indeed the destination, for Route 66 across New Mexico reminds us at once how far we have come and how much we have lost along the way.

—Marti Niman

Stepping Beyond One's Limits

When I was 13 years old, I rode my horse for the first time in a barrels competition at the Quay County Fair just off Route 66 in Tucumcari. I recall showing up at the arena in my worn jeans with my dusty ranch horse and seeing the other girls dressed in orchid and scarlet cowboy hats with matching suede chaps and horses groomed so they shone. Intimidated though I was, I ran those barrels with my whole heart.

I didn't win or even place in the competition, and I never felt the need to do it again. But the experience was revelatory for me because it pushed me beyond my comfort limits. I've had similar experiences all along Route 66. In Santa Rosa's Blue Hole, I got my scuba diving certification, plunging down some 60 feet into the icy water. Not far from Grants, I did my first cave descent. Wearing a helmet with a light attached, we climbed into lava tubes where we encountered pure darkness and clear blue ice.

The courage to step beyond one's limits defined the whole Route 66 experience. During the Great Depression, travelers set out to find

Above: Travel into a simulated uranium mine at the Grants Mining Museum.

Opposite, below: Many of the pots made at Acoma Pueblo feature geometric patterns.

new lives on that ribbon of highway stretching west. And though today we often associate Route 66 with its remnants such as neon signs, diners and court motels, the true route had to do with the vital life of the West, where cowboys and Indians lived in ways considered unconventional in the East.

That quality is still very much alive. Driving along it we may stop to watch a bronc ride at a rodeo or dive off a cliff into the Blue Hole. We may travel down into a replica mine in Grants, observe an Acoma potter at work on the Sky City mesa top, or see a Zuni Olla Dance in Gallup. Such experiences may challenge us, but more importantly, they bring us into the present moment, where we meet our own true road warrior.

CORRALES ROAD...

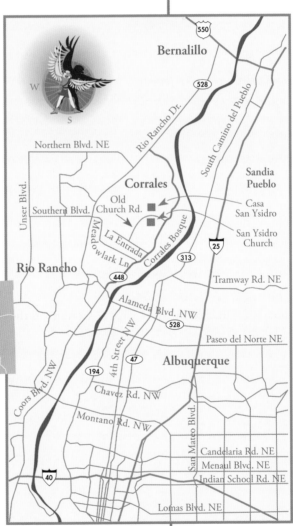

Bernalillo

550

528

Rio Rancho Dr.

South Camino del Pueblo

Northern Blvd. NE

Sandia
Pueblo

Corrales

Unser Blvd.

Southern Blvd.

Old
Church Rd.

Casa
San Ysidro

La Entrada

San Ysidro
Church

Meadowlark Ln.

Corrales Bosque

Rio Rancho

448

313

25

Tramway Rd. NE

Alameda Blvd. NW

528

Paseo del Norte NE

4th Street NW

47

194

Albuquerque

Coors Blvd. NW

Chavez Rd. NW

Montano Rd. NW

San Mateo Blvd.

Candelaria Rd. NE

Menaul Blvd. NE

40

Indian School Rd. NE

Lomas Blvd. NE

Be sure to drive the Corrales Road Scenic Byway with
your windows rolled down. Better yet, walk.

Listen to the sounds of birds in the bosque and water in the acequia. Breathe in the earthy smells of livestock and tilled earth—and
roasting green chile in the fall. Revel in the lush greenness of the best
remaining example of the middle Río Grande cottonwood forest.
Experience an oasis of rural life in the middle of the busy metropolitan
Albuquerque area.

The beginning of the byway looks like a busy intersection in any
large city, complete with heavy traffic and shopping centers on every
corner. But as you drive north, things begin to change. A sign pro-
hibits trucks over five tons on Corrales Road. Another sign suggests:
"Drive slow, see our village. Drive fast, see our judge." A truck pulling
a huge load of hay sits by the road. Goats, geese, cattle, horses and
ostriches wander around property enclosed by split-rail fences.

The old Corrales acequia, excavated in the early 18th century, parallels the road on the west side, and the Río Grande parallels the road on
the east. This surfeit of water makes the area greener and lusher than
is usual in New Mexico. The Río Grande feeds the Corrales Bosque,
which was annexed by the Village of Corrales in the 1970s and later
declared a nature preserve. The bosque's 400 acres along 10 miles of
the river provide habitat for more than 180 species of migrating and
nesting birds. Trails through the bosque offer places to exercise for
walkers, joggers, bicyclists and horse-
back riders. Bird watching and fishing are also favorite activities.

Tiwa Indians inhabited and
farmed this area long before it

Opposite, inset: A carreta *(cart)
at Casa San Ysidro in Corrales
reflects the area's Hispanic roots.*

Photo by Dan Monaghan

A rainbow colors the sky in rural Corrales.

Photo by Steve Larese

became known as Los Corrales de Alameda. They practiced irrigated agriculture as long as 1,300 years ago. Corrales was established on part of the 106,274-acre Alameda Land Grant, given to Corporal Francisco Montes y Vigil in 1710 for his role in the reconquest of New Mexico. Spanish law required Vigil to live on the grant, and since he was unable to, he sold it to Captain Juan José Gonzales Bas in 1712. The extensive corrals that Captain Gonzales built here gave the settlement its name.

You may notice vineyards along the byway. In the 1860s, Italian and French farming families began to settle in Corrales. By the 1880s, a French family was successfully growing several varieties of grapes. Corrales was known for its vineyards by 1900. You may also notice that the land has been divided into long, narrow plots. By Spanish tradition, and necessitated by the arid climate, all heirs received land with access to the irrigation ditch. Through subsequent generations, the plots became increasingly narrow.

San Ysidro, the patron saint of farmers, is also the patron saint of Corrales. The San Ysidro Church at 804 Old Church Road was built after the Iglesia Jesús, María y José was destroyed by a flood in 1868. A second San Ysidro Church was constructed in 1961, and the old one was desanctified. It began a slow decline, helped along by a fire and the use of the building as a theater. The Corrales Historical Society rescued it in 1974 and began its restoration in 1987. It is again a meeting place for the community, used for public events and concerts, and represents a classic example of a 19th-century Hispanic New Mexican village church.

Casa San Ysidro, part of the Albuquerque Museum, is just across the road from the old church, at 973 Old Church Road. Tours are available to the public during limited hours. The Gutierrez family, early settlers in the area, built a hacienda here around 1875 that was no longer standing when Alan and Shirley Minge purchased the property in 1953. The Minges decided to create a reproduction of a Spanish Colonial hacienda on the still-existing foundation. The house contains architectural details and construction techniques dating from the early 1600s through the Territorial Period in the 1800s. It houses a collection of rare Hispanic New Mexican artifacts.

Savor a slower pace of life on the Corrales Road Scenic Byway. Be charmed by the vestiges of Spanish Colonial life in Corrales. Come away refreshed by the respite from city traffic and bustle. Enjoy.

—Laurie Evans Frantz

TURQUOISE
TRAIL . . .

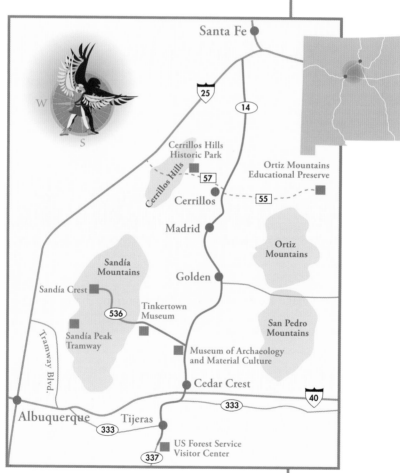

Santa Fe

25

14

Cerrillos Hills
Historic Park

Cerrillos Hills

57

Ortiz Mountains
Educational Preserve

55

Cerrillos

Madrid

Ortiz
Mountains

Sandía
Mountains

Golden

Sandía Crest

536

Tinkertown
Museum

San Pedro
Mountains

Tramway Blvd.

Sandía Peak
Tramway

Museum of Archaeology
and Material Culture

Cedar Crest

40

333

Albuquerque

Tijeras

333

337

US Forest Service
Visitor Center

W

S

Follow the high road — not the highway — between Santa Fe and Albuquerque, and trace the trail forged centuries ago by Native Americans, miners and Spanish *conquistadores.*

The Turquoise Trail National Scenic Byway winds through rustic villages as quirky as the goblinesque rock formations that jut from its roadside. This 52-mile backway offers a glimpse of life modes, both past and present, which are far removed from the flat line of the interstate.

Named for the rich turquoise deposits found in the area, the Turquoise Trail quickly launches travelers into the wild and wooly West, just south of Santa Fe, where it passes a herd of resident buffalo. Known officially as N.M. 14, the trail carves through piñon, juniper and bizarre rock outcrops sheltering both rough-hewn and futuristic off-the-grid homes. A short jaunt west on Santa Fe C.R. 57 leads to the dirt streets and adobe houses of Cerrillos, established in 1879 as a tent camp within the Cerrillos Mining District. A combination trading post, petting zoo and mining museum, Casa Grande Trading Post displays everything from live llamas to lapidary tools. Along the quiet streets of the village are art studios, galleries, antique shops, a café, a church and possibly a passing cowboy on horseback or a small herd of sheep.

From Cerrillos, drive about a half-mile to the 1,100-acre Cerrillos Hills State Park, one of the oldest mining areas in North America. Turquoise mining dates from at least A.D. 900 and the blue-green stones found their way to Chaco

Opposite, inset: The charming village of Cerrillos welcomes visitors.

Photo by Dan Monaghan, N.M. Tourism Department

Canyon, the crown jewels of old Spain and likely Chichen Itza and Monte Alban in Mexico. The hills were a source of lead used for glaze paint by Río Grande Pueblo potters from A.D. 1300 to A.D. 1700. Gold-hungry Spanish explorers settled for its galena silver lodes between 1598 and 1846. Santa Fe County Open Space now runs the park as a hiking, biking and equestrian area. A kiosk at the entrance boasts a noon analemma—a figure-eight sundial marking the sun's path as it shines through the aperture of the "infosculpture."

The 1,350-acre Ortiz Mountains Educational Preserve is a spectacular high-desert geological and natural area about two miles east of N.M. 14 on Santa Fe C.R. 55. Owned by the Santa Fe Botanical Garden, the area is open for guided hikes by advance reservation only. In the coal mining town-cum-artist's colony of Madrid, visitors might best park their cars and venture on foot, offering a better view of the quirky and fanciful clapboard homes and company stores descended from its mining era. Gilt angels, iron elk, Stonehenge gates and old gas pumps encircle fountains and rock gardens.

Dating from the town's mining heyday of the early 1800s, the buildings now house artisan shops, galleries and sculpture gardens. Once a boomtown mining both hard and soft coal from shafts dropping 2,500 feet, Madrid supplied coal for the Santa Fe Railroad, local consumers and the U.S. government. Today, the town hosts music festivals in the ballpark. Locals and visitors congregate at a tavern and a wood-planked country store.

As the road slices through tiny Golden, capricious sculptures of welded steel wildlife and twisted geometric prisms adorn hills and homes. The Ortiz Mountains dominate the

Opposite: Ride the Sandía Peak Tram for a bird's-eye view of Albuquerque.

Photo by Dan Monaghan, N.M. Tourism Department

eastern horizon, mere stumps of their former volcanic glory. Some 29 million years ago, these mountains likely resembled Mount Fuji at more than twice their current height, now eroded by wind and water into pillowy hills.

Several miles south, the Turquoise Trail curls up N.M. 536 through the wooded Cíbola National Forest to the 10,678-foot summit of Sandía Crest. Vast vistas stretch westward across the desert floor to

Albuquerque, the Río Grande and sacred Mount Taylor beyond. Intrepid visitors may get the urge to leap into the spiked granite cliffs below, but there is no need for such extreme adventures. The Sandía Peak Tram accommodates that urge with a 15-minute lift that travels 3,819 feet across four life zones—from the Hudsonian at the top to the Sonoran at the 6,500-foot base. Sandía means watermelon in Spanish and the jagged peaks turn vibrant pink at dusk, defining the skyline of Albuquerque below. For those who prefer terra firma, a restaurant, observation deck and information center are clustered near the tram deck.

Above and opposite: The late Ross Ward carved all of the intricate Western town displays at Tinkertown Museum.

Photos by Steve Larese

Returning to the offbeat world of N.M. 14, Tinkertown Museum is an oddball treasure trove displaying 40 years of one man's hand-carved wooden miniatures. A Western town springs to life with rowdy, animated characters while a three-ring circus shelters the fat lady and a teeter-totter polar bear. On a more erudite note, the Museum of Archaeology and Material Culture in Cedar Crest offers a 12,000-year timeline relating the story of North America's earliest inhabitants through the 1890 Battle of Wounded Knee.

N.M. 14 ducks under I-40 into Tijeras, the southern gateway of the Turquoise Trail, where travelers may visit the Cíbola National Forest Sandía Ranger District for maps and additional information. Shops and restaurants abound in both Tijeras and Cedar Crest to refresh travelers before their highway re-entry through Tijeras Canyon and urban Albuquerque beyond.

—Laurie Evans Frantz

An Intimate Art Journey

A s I drive along the Turquoise Trail Scenic Byway, I see art every-where. Certainly, the natural world presents many masterpieces: the vertical beds of pink and ivory sandstone at the Garden of the Gods, the elegantly rounded Cerrillos Hills, and the robust pyramidal Ortiz Mountains, but human-made art prevails as well.

Creative people have lived along the Trail for centuries, dating back to Native Americans who settled here and mined turquoise in the hills. But only since the early 1970s did a real art movement begin, unlocking the door for the rest of us to take home the bounti-ful beauty.

Diana and Mel Johnson were at the forefront of the movement. In 1973, they came from the Art Institute of Chicago to Madrid, where they opened their gallery, Johnsons of Madrid, in what was once the old Huber Motor Company, the mechanical shop for the coal mine that operated here from the late 1800s to the 1950s. "Madrid was like a ghost town when we came," says Diana. In fact, the Huber family had tried to sell it whole for $250,000, but failed.

Other artists and craftspeople moved in during the '70s as well, and they continue to come, the range of styles always broadening. Much of the art along the Trail is made in the region, which is what's most distinctive about the experience of traveling here. While I shop, I visit with artists and learn about their processes.

I meet a jewelry maker who fashions stone and chain necklaces, a sculptor who carves "anorexic angels" from thin cottonwood branch-es, and painter who depicts moody trees against a saffron sky. Best of all, in nearby Cerrillos, at the Casa Grande Trading Post, I meet owners Todd and Patricia Brown, who in the nearby Cerrillos Hills, mine nature's own jewelry that I can take home: turquoise.

Above: Brightly colored storefronts beckon visitors to shop in the Gypsy Plaza in Madrid.

Below: A variety of turquoise can be found at the Casa Grande Trading Post in Cerrillos.

MESALANDS . . .

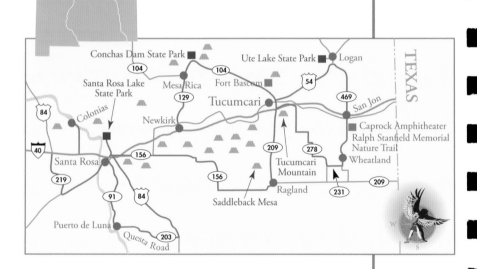

Conchas Dam State Park

Ute Lake State Park — Logan

TEXAS

104

104

Santa Rosa Lake State Park

Mesa Rica

Fort Bascom

54

129

Tucumcari

469

San Jon

84

Colonias

Newkirk

Caprock Amphitheater
Ralph Stanfield Memorial
Nature Trail

40

209

278

156

Tucumcari
Mountain

Wheatland

Santa Rosa

156

Ragland

209

219

231

91

84

Saddleback Mesa

Puerto de Luna

203

Questa Road

W

S

One morning, 150 million years ago, a 3-foot-long, meat-eating dinosaur walked to the edge of a large inland sea for refreshment. It was to be his last drink of water.

The dinosaur would have been forgotten forever if his remains had not been discovered long after his death in Quay County. He would come to be known as *Allosaurus*.

Mesalands Scenic Byway is about dinosaurs. The banks of the sea that *Allosaurus* walked along are now the edges of the mesas in northeastern New Mexico. The term mesa implies something square and straight-sided, but up close, mesas are anything but tidy. Huge tabular rocks project out from their rims; their slopes are littered with big rock slabs.

Dinosaurs roamed Quay County during the Triassic, Jurassic and Cretaceous periods, and bands of color in the mesas represent these eras. The red rocks and soil at the bottom remain from the Triassic Era. The most dramatic example of this period can be seen driving north on N.M. 129 from Newkirk. Huge red boulders are strewn over the red ground. The layer from the Jurassic Period varies from cream to gray, and the Cretaceous Period is the cream-colored stratum on top.

South of San Jon, N.M. 469 climbs to the top of the mesalands.

The entrance to the Caprock Amphitheatre and Ralph Stanfield Memorial Nature Trail is to the left at the top of the mesa. A paved trail leads to the edge of the caprock, where the modern Tertiary Period topsoil covers the Cretaceous sandstone. At this transition point, you may see marine fossils. There are piles of fossilized oyster shells on some of these mesas.

Opposite, below and inset: Mesalands Dinosaur Museum in Tucumcari showcases bronze casts of dinosaur bones.

Photo by Steve Larese

Conchas Lake at Conchas Dam State Park offers fishing, boating and camping.

Photo by Dan Monaghan, N.M. Tourism Department

The story of this area's ancient history is told at Mesalands Dinosaur Museum in Tucumcari. The museum is part of Mesalands Community College and casts dinosaur remains in bronze at the school's Fine Arts Bronze Foundry. Bronze shows every detail of the original bone. Even the tiny serrations on a *Tyrannosaurus Rex* tooth are clearly visible. The museum houses the world's largest collection of bronze dinosaur replicas.

Mesalands Scenic Byway is about exploration. In May 1541, Spanish explorer Francisco Vasquez de Coronado and his expedition camped along the west bank of the Pecos River for four days while building a bridge across it. A small community, Puerto de Luna, was established there by the early 1860s. Its name, "gateway to the moon," is as enchanting as a drive through it. Driving south on N.M. 91 from Santa Rosa, small mesas point their noses toward the road, hovering protectively over the Pecos River Valley. The road winds inconspicuously through the valley, following the contours of the land.

What makes Puerto de Luna so charming? The winding Pecos River Valley lined with big, gnarly cottonwood trees, the acequias, the illusion that life here is as it was 100 years ago, the old adobe and stone buildings. Puerto de Luna was the Guadalupe County seat from 1891 until 1903. The courthouse still stands but has lost its roof. Alexander Grzelachowski, a merchant in Territorial New Mexico, ran a store here. His plastered-stone home still stands in the middle of town. On the east side of the river is Nuestra Señora de Refugio Catholic Church, constructed in 1882. On the west side is tiny Santa Inez Church, next door to a house with windows set deep in thick, bright turquoise walls. Buttresses support its corners. Places like this contribute to the magic of Puerto de Luna.

Colonias, nestled in the mesas northwest of Santa Rosa, is also a small town lost in time. The yellow stucco on the San José Church has fallen off to reveal the melted contours of red adobe bricks. There are more dead cars than houses, and more empty houses than inhabited ones.

The Spanish explorer Antonio de Espejo passed through the Santa Rosa area in 1590. He may have passed by Tucumcari Mountain, long a landmark for travelers along the Canadian River. Explorer Pedro Vial mentioned it in 1793, while opening a trail between Santa Fe and St. Louis, and Captain Randolph Marcy led an expedition past it in 1849.

Mesalands Scenic Byway is about Comanches. Having acquired the horse, the Comanche Indians started moving into this area in the 1700s. They were involved in conflicts with Indian, Spanish and Anglo settlers for more than a century. Fort Bascom was built in 1863 to protect settlers from Comanche raids. A sign on N.M. 104 marks its location, but the fort no longer stands. The Tucumcari Historical Museum has an exhibit of artifacts from the fort.

Kit Carson and General Philip Sheridan led campaigns against the Comanches in the 1860s. Fort Bascom was abandoned in 1870, but the Comanches were not defeated until 1874. A permanent settlement, Liberty, was finally established in the area at about this time. With the arrival of the railroad in 1898, Liberty moved eight miles south to form Tucumcari. Driving south on N.M. 104, Tucumcari's classic railroad depot is visible to the west as you enter town. A block south of the depot is the community's vintage downtown.

Mesalands Scenic Byway is about outlaws. Black Jack Ketchum, the last of the train robbers, frequented this area. In the 1880s, Black Jack killed two men south of Tucumcari (a sign on N.M. 209 commemorates the deed) and hid out near Saddleback Mesa. Ketchum was wounded in the 1899 robbery of a train, which had been held up twice before. The fed-up conductor shot the outlaw in the elbow, almost severing his arm. This led to his arrest shortly thereafter and his hanging in 1901.

Billy the Kid had many friends in Puerto de Luna and patronized Alexander Grzelachowski's general store. He ate his last Christmas dinner at Grzelachowski's house as Pat Garrett's prisoner in 1880. On July 14, 1881, Sheriff Pat Garrett killed him in Fort Sumner. A street in Puerto de Luna, Kid Lane, commemorates his connection with the village.

Mesalands Scenic Byway is about lakes. Ute Lake, Santa Rosa Lake and Conchas Dam state parks are all along his byway. They offer fishing, camping and picnicking. Santa Rosa, known as the City of Natural Lakes, is famous for scuba diving in the middle of the desert. Blue Hole, a natural, 80-foot-deep pool, is a mecca for

The Blue Hole at Santa Rosa draws divers from all over the world.

Photo by Dan Monaghan, N.M. Tourism Department

divers. Santa Rosa is also home to Janes-Wallace Dam Lake, Park Lake and Perch Lake.

Mesalands Scenic Byway is about solitude. As I drive north on N.M. 278, the setting sun highlights the brilliant bands of red, cream and tan on the mesa slopes. New Mexico has many roads like those that make up Mesalands Scenic Byway— paved or unpaved, through miles and miles of open land. Each road is a new experience and a new gift—of beauty, solitude and adventure.

—Laurie Evans Frantz

Friendly Greetings Along the Byway

Though this region is most known for Historic Route 66 neon, its true heart shines far brighter, and that becomes clear when traveling the Mesalands Scenic Byway. It's shaped by the wide open spaces, which engender friendly hearts.

In Tucumcari I meet up with one of them. Scooter Mitchell comes from a long line of ranchers in the region. An attorney who received his Bachelor of Arts degree at Stanford, he chose to settle in this town of some 6,000 residents. Over steaming plates of burritos in the Main Street Historic District, he explains why. "I enjoy knowing a lot of people," he says, stopping to chat with a few passersby. "The downside is, you know a lot of people." He smiles and explains that all the friendliness appeals to him, but when he goes out to eat, it's hard to get a bite in.

After lunch, Scooter tours me around this historic district, which is in the midst of a revitalization. In the early 1900s it was the center of activity and still retains graceful buildings from that era. We step into a few galleries, where locals sell a range of art. We admire the 1936 Art Deco neon of the Odeon Theater, now open for first-run movies, and marvel at the Misson Style Tucumcari Train Depot, which is being made into an arts center. Throughout it all we pass murals depicting the town's history and the same gracious spirit that has pervaded the day.

In Santa Rosa, my guide is the mayor, José Campos. He tours me on his bright yellow Victory motorcycle first to what he calls PDL—Puerto de Luna—a village where his family originated. Long meadows bordering the Pecos River roll out beside us as José banks on the curving road, pointing out to me places he's known since childhood. "This is our pilgrimage," he says over the sound of the wind. "So

The Pecos River shimmers as it flows near Puerto de Luna.

many of us are from here that we drive this road—like (it's) the road home." Finches flit up from ditch banks and the motorcycle engine rumbles beneath us.

On the way back, José takes me around Santa Rosa, a city of some 2,750 residents that was founded in the 1860s. We cruise past vintage signs on Route 66—La Mesa and Sun 'n Sand motels, and Joseph's Bar and Grill—owned by José, the mayor himself. As a grand finale, we circle through Old Town, a place that's now seeing a revitalization, with antique street lamps and a renovated court-house and city hall. Nearly everyone we pass waves, the region's friendly spirit ever-present.

SALT
MISSIONS
TRAIL . . .

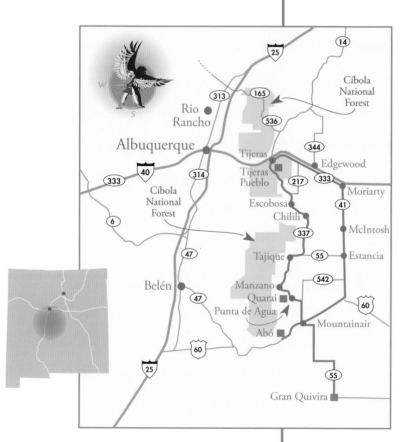

25
14
Cíbola
National
Forest
313
165
536
Rio
Rancho
Albuquerque
Tijeras
344
Edgewood
40
Tijeras
Pueblo
333
314
217
333
Moriarty
333
Cíbola
National
Forest
Escobosa
41
Chilili
6
McIntosh
337
47
Tajique
55
Estancia
542
Belén
Manzano
47
Quarai
60
Punta de Agua
60
Abó
Mountainair
60
25
55
Gran Quivira

The Salt Missions Trail Scenic Byway traverses the heart of New Mexico, from the mountains to the plains. It follows old trade routes, rail beds and footpaths that echo with the hazy activities of yesteryear.

If you listen closely, you'll hear the footsteps of Indians trading life's necessities, the whistle of a train as it pulls into the station or the chattering voices of families traveling across the country on Route 66.

The byway starts at the junction of N.M. 337 and N.M. 333 in Tijeras Canyon, which links the Sandía and Manzano mountains as well as eastern New Mexico with the Río Grande Valley. Tijeras was the site of a large pueblo from the 1200s until 1435. The archaeological site is now administered by the Cíbola National Forest. A free, self-guided tour wanders through its 80 rooms. Tijeras Canyon has long been an important travel corridor. It provided an east-west passage between the Sandía and Manzano mountains. Apaches traveled through the canyon to raid communities along the Río Grande. Later, Hispanic settlers used the canyon for timber and game and as a trading route.

Between Tijeras and Moriarty, the byway shares the road with Route 66 National Scenic Byway. Now known as N.M. 333, the old route is commemorated on the signs of many modern businesses. Some original Route 66 architecture remains, but the spirit of Route 66 lives on in the many modern family-operated businesses along the old route.

The eastern and southern branches of the byway run through the plains, while its western branch traverses the mountains. Edgewood, about halfway between Tijeras and Moriarty,

Opposite, inset: This church in Tajique is one of many along the Salt Missions Trail Scenic Byway.

Photo by James Orr

93

The ruins of San Buenaventura Mission at Gran Quivira remind us of the massive church that was here in 1659.

Photo by James Orr

is on the very edge of the mountains, as its name implies. By the time you reach Moriarty, you are definitely on flat land. Moriarty has historically been an important link in transportation corridors. It was named after an early settler seeking a cure for rheumatism who settled there in 1887. In 1901, it became a stop on the New Mexico Central Railroad, which was built between Santa Fe and Torrance counties. When Route 66 was realigned in 1938, it ran through Moriarty; now Moriarty can be accessed via an exit off I-40.

The byway follows N.M. 41 south out of Moriarty. It runs through McIntosh and Estancia, both of which were stops on the New Mexico Central, before turning west on U.S. 60. McIntosh was a shipping cen-

Mountainair still reflects its rural roots, while also supporting a growing arts community.

Photo by Dan Monaghan, N.M. Tourism Department

ter on the railroad for wool, lumber, flour and pinto beans. Estancia, which means "small farm" or "resting place," is the seat of Torrance County. The town is distinguished by its spring-fed pond, a haven for ducks and geese.

The next community on the byway is Mountainair, founded in 1902. Mountainair was known as "the pinto bean capital of the world" until the drought of the 1940s. It is now an attractive community with small shops and charming architecture. The local burrito joint is painted bright red and yellow with a mural on the front, and even the façade of the police department/municipal court is decorated with Southwestern designs. But Clem "Pop" Shaffer, an early settler who combined his building skills with unparalleled whimsy, built the most interesting structures. You have to see them to appreciate them. Both Rancho Bonito (1937) and the Shaffer Hotel (1923) are adorned with colorful Southwestern symbols and Shaffer's distinctive anthropomorphic animal designs in stone, concrete and wood.

Mountainair is the starting point for the places that gave this byway its name: the ruins of Abó (nine miles west on U.S. 60), Quarai (eight miles north on N.M. 55) and Gran Quivira (25 miles south on N.M. 55) pueblos. They are units of the Salinas Pueblo Missions National Monument, and a visitor center in Mountainair features a video and museum that interpret them. The pueblos lie within the Estancia Basin, which was a lake until about 10,000 years ago. When the brackish water evaporated, salt was left behind, a valuable trade commodity for later settlers. This area alternated between peace and war: Pueblo Indians against Apaches, and both against Spanish settlers. In the peaceful interludes, trade routes ran through the basin between the pueblos of the Río Grande and Plains tribes. The people of the Salinas pueblos traded salt, corn, piñon nuts, beans, squash and cotton with their neighbors.

Each of these sites has its own special beauty. The red stone walls of Abó's San Gregorio Mission (late 1620s) and Quarai's La Purísima Concepción (1630) rise up suddenly against a deep-blue sky cushioned by massive cumulus clouds. By contrast, the ruins of San Buenaventura Mission (1659) at Gran Quivira are gradually revealed as you walk to the top of Chupadero Mesa. The gray, stone walls blend with the muted colors of the desert but still contrast with the piercing blue sky.

N.M. 55 and N.M. 337 pass through several small settlements with lyrical Spanish names on their way north to Tijeras: Manzano, Tajique, Chilili, Escobosa and Yrisarri. Each of these communities has an intriguing history, and each is built around its small Catholic church.

Quarai's La Purísima Concepción was built in 1630.

Photo by James Orr

The churches differ in appearance, but their importance to the lives of the communities is the same.

Like icing on a cake, there are hiking, picnicking and camping opportunities in the lovely forested valleys of the Cíbola National Forest south of Tijeras. Take your pick amongst Tunnel Canyon, Otero Canyon, Cedro Campground and Pine Flat Picnic Area. The forest has seen many a traveler pass through before you—some of them hurrying from one place to another, some of them hunting for the necessities of life. Some of them just enjoying the serenity and beauty of the Salt Missions Trail.

—Laurie Evans Frantz

The Cibola National Forest offers great opportunities for hiking and camping along the Salt Missions Trail Scenic Byway.

Photo by James Orr

Opposite: Alpacas are the source for yarn sold during the East Mountain Fiber Farm and Studio Tour in Edgewood, near the Salt Missions Trail.

Photo by Lesley S. King

Festivals Inspire Creativity

W hen I travel to New Mexico towns I always search for what the people most love; often the answer leads me to a deeper understanding of my own and others' lives. Along the Salt Missions Trail Scenic Byway I've gotten to see—through festivals—the region's most beloved passions.

In the spring, during the East Mountain Fiber Farm and Studio Tour in Edgewood, I spend the day traveling from farm to farm, to see all manner of animals. At Milagro Moon Ranch I meet Jim and Cynthia Daly, who against the backdrop of the 8,750-foot San Pedro Mountains, raise 17 alpacas.

The sweet-natured creatures have ET eyes and an odd hum emitting from their lips. They provide just what the Dalys need in farm animals. "We wanted ones that you could get the product from without ending their lives," says Jim. The Dalys sell the yarn in shades ranging from white to tan to black, as well as items made from it, including scarves, dolls and felted wall hangings.

The following hours are filled with similar treats as I visit the 10 farms along the route. I learn that fiber animals such as alpacas, llamas, sheep and rabbits are comfortable here because of the mild climate. I pet a camel, see a peacock preen, and even watch as yarn is

spun directly from the back of an English angora rabbit. The spinner assures me it doesn't hurt him at all.

Farther along the Salt Missions Trail, another town celebrates a different connection to the natural world. The Mountainair Sunflower Festival in August holds the brilliantly smiling bloom up for appreciation.

During the festival, I find sunflowers everywhere. At the community center, booths hold local art ranging from refrigerator magnets to hand-made cards to painted gourds, all with sunflower motifs. Most notable is a soulful *retablo* of Santa Teresa holding a bouquet of the happy blossoms.

The local co-op gallery presents a "Sunflower Power" exhibit. As well as sunflower sconces, I see moody pastels and striking photos. Contributing to the fun are works on paper by local elementary school kids. As I walk the main street, listening to a teenager busk rock music, I find kids' art in almost every business window: sunflowers fashioned of construction paper, crayons and magazine clippings.

Of course all around town and in the meadows beyond, the brilliance glows each August, with nature-made sunflowers everywhere. It's no wonder these people are so inspired. The beauty along this byway encourages me to let my own creativity shine.

Opposite, inset: Piñon trees dot the landscape surrounding the Abó Pass Trail.

Photo by Dan Monaghan, N.M. Tourism Department

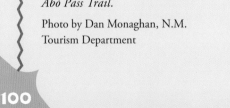

ABO PASS
TRAIL . . .

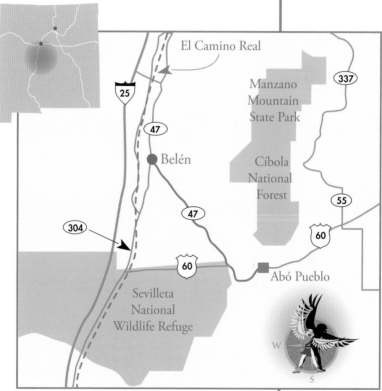

El Camino Real

Manzano
Mountain
State Park

337

25

47

Belén

Cíbola
National
Forest

55

47

304

60

60

Abó Pueblo

Sevilleta
National
Wildlife Refuge

W

S

Fray Francisco de Acevedo founded San Gregorio de Abó Mission in 1629.

Photo by Mike Stauffer, N.M.
Tourism Department

Around 1540, small bands of Pueblo Indians trudged east through the Río Grande Valley, carrying maize, piñon nuts, beans, squash and cotton goods, to trade with their Plains Indian neighbors.

In return, they expected to receive dried buffalo meat, hides, flints, shells and salt. The route these traders took led past the Pueblo of Abó, strategically located near a cluster of springs on the trail to Abó Pass. This old footpath is now the Abó Pass Trail Scenic Byway.

The byway links El Camino Real National Scenic Byway and the Salt Missions Trail Scenic Byway. It starts on the east side of Belén, where N.M. 47 angles off to the southeast towards its junction with U.S. 60. The byway follows U.S. 60 east for twelve miles to Abó Pueblo. With Gran Quivira and Quarai, Abó is now part of Salinas Pueblo Missions National Monument.

Driving down the byway from Belén, the grass-carpeted plains of the Río Grande Valley stretch into the distance. As the byway turns east onto U.S. 60, the road starts to climb the foothills of the Manzanos, and the terrain changes to red rock formations scattered with piñon and juniper. Pull over and look back at the wide expanse of the plains, framed on the northeast by the Manzano Mountains. The Sevilleta National Wildlife Refuge unfolds to the west. Wildlife at Sevilleta includes desert bighorn sheep, pronghorn, mule deer, mountain lion, bear and bird species, including golden eagle, roadrunner, wood duck, heron and burrowing owl. A visitor center and a portion of the refuge are open to the public for hiking, observing wildlife and seasonal hunting.

Members of don Juan de Oñate's expedition in 1598 visited this area. The land grant of Nuestra Señora de Belén (Our Lady of Bethlehem) was established on El Camino Real in 1740, and was

Above: The massive stone walls of San Gregorio de Abó Mission have survived for more than 300 years.

Opposite: Migrating sandhill cranes can sometimes be spotted in the region.

Photos: James Orr

settled by Captain Diego de Torres and 32 others. With the coming of the Americans in 1846, immigrants began to stream into the area, and Belén developed as a mercantile center. In 1880, the railroad entered Belén, and the Homestead Act of 1889 brought more hardy pioneers to central New Mexico. At the turn of the century, the Atchison, Topeka and Santa Fe Railway was looking for a new route over the mountains of New Mexico. The AT&SF Railway built a bypass, the Belén Cutoff, from Belén to Texico over Abó Pass. Thereafter, all transcontinental freight trains were routed through Belén to refuel and change crews. The latest improvement to the Abó Pass trade route was the construction of the modern paved roads of N.M. 47 and U.S. 60.

Trains travel with you all along this byway, whether you're crossing the tracks, you're driving next to them, or you're watching them recede into the distance. The tracks would seem to stretch into infinity if they didn't disappear into the Abó Pass. Driving up the hill toward Abó, the jagged, red stone walls of San Gregorio de Abó Mission loom up through the trees. In contrast, only unexcavated mounds of melted adobe mark the extensive pueblo room blocks. One of the Southwest's largest Pueblo villages, Abó was inhabited from the 1300s until the 1670s. In the Piro language, *abo* is thought to mean "water bowl," or perhaps "poor" or "poor place."

The Salinas Pueblos are named for the salt flats and shallow, brackish lakes in the Estancia Valley, remnants of a large lake that filled the Estancia Basin as recently as 10,000 years ago. Don Juan de Oñate called salt one of the four riches of New Mexico. Drought forced Indians from the Salinas area to move to other pueblos in the 1670s. During the Pueblo Revolt in 1680, they went south to the El Paso area with the Spanish, intermingling with other Pueblo refugees.

The people who forged the Abó Pass Trail could not foresee the future importance of their humble footpath. Today's travelers sometimes forget that they owe their ease of travel to these early beginnings.

—Laurie Evans Frantz

Belén's Generous Spirit

A perfect way to get a feel of the history and life around the Abó Pass Trail Scenic Byway is to start the adventure in Belén. This town of 8,000 residents, settled in the 1700s as the Belén Land Grant, shares its name with the place of Christ's birth, Bethlehem. It has a hospitable spirit that one would anticipate with such a name.

At the heart of town stands a grand stucco structure, the Harvey House Museum. In the late 1800s, restauranteur Fred Harvey built a chain of railroad hotels and dining rooms, which spread elegant hospitality across the West. This one, in business from 1910 to 1939, still resides on a thriving railyard, one of the busiest on the Burlington Northern Santa Fe line, with some 80 trains passing by each day.

Inside the Harvey House Museum I find artifacts from the Harvey House days and Belén's history. These include exhibits of the legendary Harvey Girls, adventuresome young women who headed west to live and work in the hotels, where they charmed travelers with their beauty and spunk. The museum displays one of their modest bedrooms and stories of real Harvey Girls who lived in Belén.

Along the main street I stop in at various shops, where I find delightful pottery, jewelry, paintings and photographs and meet a few of the artists. Cheri Reckers, who creates plush fiber pillows and wall-hangings, finds the nature surrounding Belén especially welcoming. "I wake to the birds chirping, the cows mooing and the sun coming up over the mountains. It's inspiring!"

Opposite, top: The Harvey House Museum in Belén tells the story of the famous Harvey Girls in its many exhibits.

Opposite, below: Cheri Reckers holds one of her artistic pillow creations.

The town's historical architecture has also invited attention. In 1996, nationally renowned artist and feminist Judy Chicago renovated the early-1900s Belén Hotel, which is on the National Register of Historic Places, to serve as her studio and home. The stately historic district where it resides has been celebrated in movies including the sweet-hearted 2008 *Swing Vote* starring Kevin Costner.

I finish my day at Pete's Café. The late Pete and Eligia Torres opened the restaurant in 1949, and today their daughter Theresa Padilla and her husband, Alfred, continue to serve some of the region's best New Mexican food. Just as I'd expect, a big plate of chicken enchiladas is served with a hospitable smile— and after such a generous day, the flavors taste like pure love.

SOCORRO HISTORICAL DISTRICT . . .

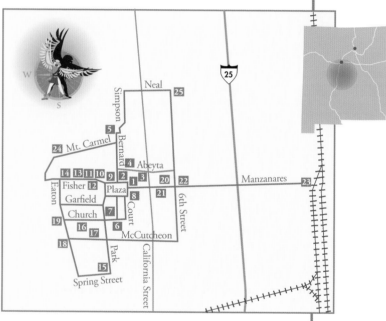

1. The Hilton Block
2. Juan Nepomuceno Garcia House
3. Garcia Opera House
4. Juan Jose Baca House
5. San Miguel Mission
6. Socorro County Courthouse
7. Court St. Historic Structures
8. Capitol Bar
9. Fitch Building
10. Crabtree Building
11. Water Department
12. Fire Department
13. Episcopal Church

14. Jesus Torres House
15. Casa de la Flecha
16. Bursum & Chambon House
17. Courtesy House
18. Eaton House
19. 303 Eaton House
20. Loma Theater
21. Knights of Pythias Hall
22. Valverde Hotel
23. AT&SF Railroad Depot
24. Stapleton House
25. Hammel Museum

The history of Socorro is told in its architecture, and the Socorro Historical District Scenic Byway is the visual embodiment of that history.

The oldest existing structure in Socorro, the San Miguel Mission, is a cornerstone of the Socorro Historical District Scenic Byway and the foundation of the town's history. A leisurely drive through Socorro's old streets will give the traveler a glimpse of its progression from a quiet colonial town, to wild mining town, to the modern settlement of today.

Two Franciscan priests, who entered New Mexico with the Don Juan de Oñate expedition in 1598, built a small church at the site of the Piro Indian Pueblo of Pilabo. This was replaced by the present building between 1615 and 1621. The Pueblo Revolt of 1680 forced the abandonment of Socorro, but the massive adobe walls, huge vigas and supporting corbel arches of the church saved it from complete collapse. When the Socorro area was finally resettled in 1815, the church was dilapidated, but the walls and beams were still standing. They are the frame of the present church.

Other buildings dating to the Spanish Colonial period still stand in Socorro, especially in the area of the mission. A good example is the adobe Juan Nepomuceno Garcia House, with its flat roof and courtyard (108 Bernard). Portions of the home may date to 1816. Another example is the house of Juan José Baca, the grandson of one of the original Socorro settlers, built at Abeyta Street and the Plaza about 1870.

Fertile land and a good water supply made Socorro a desirable place

Opposite, inset: A gazebo provides the focal point for festivities on the Plaza.

Photo by Mike Stauffer, N.M. Tourism Department

to settle and, by the late 1850s, about 600 people lived there. The population grew gradually until the 1860s, when lead and silver were discovered in the nearby Magdalena Mountains. With the arrival of the railroad in the 1880s, Socorro became a wild boomtown, growing to more than 4,000 people. Miners and business people flocked to the town to make their fortunes. Many of the buildings on the byway date to this period, including the Opera House Garcia built at the corner of Terry Avenue and California in 1886. Many famous performers appeared at the Garcia Opera House in the late 19th and early 20th centuries, and it was the site of social events such as dances, political rallies, marriages and basketball games. Socorro's largest brick dwelling, La Casa de la Flecha (the House of the Arrow, named after the weathervane on the roof), was built the same year (407 Park Street).

The French Quarter (Park-Church-McCutcheon streets), one of the most affluent areas in town during this era, is still the place to see elegant homes. The Bursum and Chambon houses (326 and 324 Church respectively) are rare examples of the Eastlake Style, and both are on the National Register of Historic Places. Holm O. Bursum was leader of the Republican Party and very politically powerful in the New Mexico Territory. E.W. Eaton, the leader of a group of vigilantes called the Committee of Justice, built a home at 403 Eaton Avenue.

Many of the commercial buildings built during the boom years are still in use. The brick Hilton Block on the east end of the Plaza, named for relatives of hotel magnate Conrad Hilton, replaced earlier adobe buildings. On Manzanares Street, east of the Plaza, the Loma Theater (107 Manzanares Avenue) and the Knights of Pythias Hall (106 Manzanares Avenue) add charm to the town. The theater was originally

The San Miguel Mission reflects Socorro's deep cultural ties to the Spanish Colonial Period.

Photo by Mike Stauffer, N.M. Tourism Department

the Price-Loewenstein Mercantile Store, built by Jewish brothers-in-law fleeing oppression in Europe. The Knights of Pythias Hall is identifiable by the Owl Cigar advertisement painted on its side.

The Hammel Museum (Neal Avenue and Sixth Street) features the history of the Illinois Brewing Company. Jacob Hammel settled in St. Louis with his friend Eberhard Anheuser, who wanted him to go into partnership in a brewery. Hammel decided to start his own brewery, the Illinois Brewing Company, instead. Anheuser's business became the Anheuser-Busch Company. Hammel's sons brought the family business to Socorro in the 1880s, where it flourished until shut down by Prohibition.

The silver crash of 1893 ended Socorro's boom years. The population dropped, and ranching and farming rose in importance as mining declined. But the town could still support a new California Mission-style hotel, the Val Verde (203 Manzanares Avenue). The hotel is almost unchanged since it was built in 1919. During the 1930s, the Works Progress Administration contributed several new buildings and many sidewalks (still marked "WPA") to the town. The Victorian courthouse was torn down and replaced with the California Mission-style building still in use today (200 Church Street). Many buildings on the Plaza and Manzanares Street, including the Hilton Block, were remodeled in the California Mission style.

Socorro's long history is illustrated on the Socorro Wheel of History. This bronze sculpture, a block north of the Plaza, tells the whole story of the original Piro Indian pueblos, the Spanish Colonial settlement, the mining boomtown and the present center of science and technology. It neatly ties together more than 400 years of history on the Socorro Historical District Scenic Byway.

—Laurie Evans Frantz

Taking the Long View

When I get busy with all the little details of my life, I sometimes lose the broad view—the truth of what's really important. That is a good time for me to head to Socorro, whose very name means "help." The town of 9,000 residents offers this gift through the broad expanses of history it presents, most experienced in close proximity to the Socorro Historical District Scenic Byway.

I start my tour at the New Mexico Institute of Mining and Technology campus, where I find its Mineral Museum. Also known as "Coronado's Treasure Chest," it is a collection established in 1898 that holds some 15,000 specimens, with 2,000 on display. I make my way though the glitter and shine of minerals and gems, including icy-blue smithsonite and many types of amethyst.

But the real wonder for me is the fossils collection, where I encounter an ominous armored herring from 55 million years ago, pressed into sandstone, and a stingray from 49 million years ago, the image so vivid the creature could still be swimming. My own life's complexities erode into nearly nothing next to the beauty and the perspective offered by these great expanses of time.

My next stop, at the center of town, is the Elfego Baca Heritage Park. Along a tree-lined walkway, I find the First Contact Socorro Wheel of History, a circular sculpture depicting the region's past from 1598, when Spanish explorer Juan de Oñate first encountered Piro Indians. The town's name came from this encounter, when the Piros gave *socorro* (help) in the form of corn.

Other stops in the park spell out the his-

The sculpture titled First Contact: Socorro Wheel of History *reflects the area's heritage.*

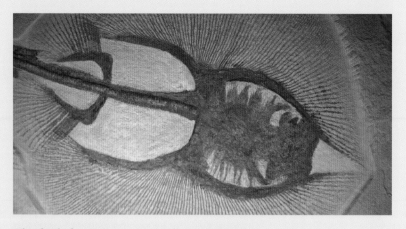

This fossil of a stingray is among the amazing trea-
sures found at the Mineral Museum on the campus of
New Mexico Institute of Mining and Technology.

tory of buildings on colorful tiles. One placard discusses the Juan
José Baca House (1870), once a store, where the folk hero Elfego Baca
worked. At that location he decided to take up arms against cowboys
down in what is now called Reserve, 150 miles to the southwest. Some
believe he brought a new order to Socorro County.

Even present-day Socorro offers inspiration for me to view my life
lightly. Though it's a small town, it still supports its own newspaper,
brewpub and coffee house. The people here have a broad life experience that permeates conversations. They include astrophysicists,
who work at the National Radio Astronomy Observatory, geologists
who teach at the New Mexico Institute of Mining and Technology,
explosives experts at the Energetic Materials Research and Testing
Center and, of course, long-time farmers and merchants.

By the time I climb in my car and head home, I'm full of a sense
that each of my little concerns is not only manageable, but also part
of the larger whole shared with courageous denizens of the cosmos.

QUEBRADAS BACK COUNTRY . . .

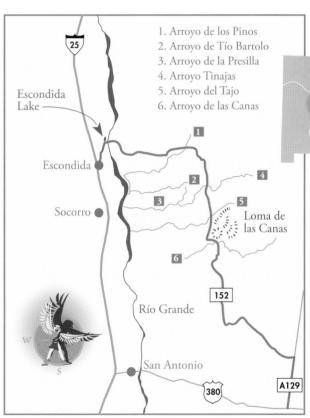

1. Arroyo de los Pinos
2. Arroyo de Tío Bartolo
3. Arroyo de la Presilla
4. Arroyo Tinajas
5. Arroyo del Tajo
6. Arroyo de las Canas

25

Escondida Lake

Escondida

Socorro

Loma de las Canas

152

Río Grande

W

S

San Antonio

380

A129

Rainbow-hued ridges, deep, jagged canyons and wind-whipped dunes await travelers wishing to venture off Interstate 25 into the rough-and-tumble geography of the Quebradas Back Country Scenic Byway.

This 24-mile unpaved road slices through the arroyos, or breaks, that give the area its Spanish name and offers both vast and intimate views of New Mexico's geologic past. Wedged between two national wildlife refuges—Sevilleta and Bosque del Apache—and the state-run Ladd S. Gordon Waterfowl Complex, the Quebradas area also offers fleeting glimpses of desert wildlife, especially at dawn and dusk.

From Interstate 25, exit at Escondida and head east, then north to the turnoff for Escondida Lake. Drive past the lake, cross the Río Grande, turn south at the "T," turn west and follow the Back Country Byway signs. The road is annually maintained. High-clearance or four-wheel-drive vehicles are recommended, although passenger cars may cross if it is dry.

This area lies along the northern edge of the upper Chihuahuan Desert, with rolling bench lands of pungent creosote scrub, Mormon tea, sand sage and four-wing saltbush punctuated by spiky yucca, cholla and prickly pear cacti. Spindly ocotillo, gray in winter and waving like upended roots, sprout bright green leaves and red-flowered tips after spring and summer rains.

Woven tapestries of yellow ochre, burnt sienna and buff-colored ridges of sandstone, shale and limestone run north-south, bisected by arroyos that drain west to the Río Grande and provide primitive camping and hiking options as well as

The Spanish term quebradas *refers to the ridges or breaks in the landscape.*

Photo by Steve Larese

117

wildlife travel corridors. Arroyos to the east and south drain into a closed basin with the ominous name Jornada del Muerto—the Journey of Death. Snow-capped Socorro Peak juts out to the west through gaps in the arroyos, while Sierra Larga, Mesa Redonda, and the orange and buff-colored cliffs of Loma de las Canas dominate horizon views along the road.

A walk into Arroyo de los Pinos at mile marker 4 reveals a rift zone of uplifted, folded and eroded layers of rock. The arroyos Tío Bartolo, Tinajas and Tajo provide sandy walkways into rocky wonderlands of vertical painted cliffs, tortured badlands and shoulder-wide box canyons. Layers of soft sedimentary rock eaten by wind and water reveal curving layers of harder rock, calling to mind dinosaur vertebrae trapped within cliffs. In some places, older rocks were faulted on top of younger rocks and layers were tilted on end or folded. Many of the red rocks are part of the same Permian Abo Formation seen on the back of the Sandía Mountains east of Albuquerque.

The region is indeed primeval. The Loma de las Canas cliffs are layered, multicolored Pennsylvanian and Permian sandstone, limestone, siltstone and shale. A Precambrian rock outcrop was carved into spectacular box canyons by the Tajo and Presilla arroyos, the limestone and granite walls sculpted by flowing water. Arroyo del Tajo shelters ancient Native American pictographs on rock walls so fragile they could crumble to dust at any moment.

Ancient seeps and springs provide oases for mule deer, jackrabbits, coyotes, bobcats, doves, quail and gray and red foxes, while some arroyos furnish wildlife travel corridors from nearby Sevilleta National Wildlife Refuge. Red-tailed, Cooper's and Swainson's hawks, American kestrels, turkey vultures, raven and numerous songbirds may be sighted as well. Wintering sandhill cranes and snow geese traverse the skies between Bosque del Apache National Wildlife Refuge to

Migrating birds can be seen along the byway.

Photo by Dan Monaghan, N.M. Tourism Department

the south and the Ladd S. Gordon Waterfowl Complex to the north. The two agencies cooperate by growing grain to attract hungry migrating birds away from local private farmlands. Travelers may see geese and cranes commuting the Río Grande waterway between the areas during the winter months. Wildlife managers mow grain low to attract geese and "bar" it to a taller height to bring in the cranes.

This is a region of solitude, stillness and expansive terrain, where time seems suspended. The song of a horned lark and the track of a roadrunner are the sole evidence of other beings. It is sometimes called "Little Utah" for its rocky resemblance to the painted desert regions of that neighboring state, but "Quebradas" is equally suitable for the rugged breaks that riffle across its badlands. The abundant arroyos tunnel into rock-strewn and twisted wonderlands for exploration on foot, while the road itself bisects an ancient land far removed from interstate bustle.

The Bureau of Land Management oversees the region for wilderness study areas, recreation, mineral exploration and livestock grazing. Photography, rock hounding, hiking, wildlife watching, hunting, cultural sightseeing and backcountry-vehicle touring are among the many recreational opportunities. The Socorro Fat Tire Festival includes the Quebradas Back Country Scenic Byway on the itinerary of its annual mountain bike race. Camping is primitive in nature, and no water or services are available along the road.

The Quebradas Back Country Scenic Byway separates the Presilla and Sierra de las Canas wilderness study areas, which are managed to preserve their natural character and primitive recreational opportunities. Travelers should plan about two or three hours to drive the road and bring water, food, a shovel and blankets. The road ends at Sandoval C.R. A129 and U.S. 380, about 11 miles east of San Antonio. Full services are available in Socorro. For more information, contact the Bureau of Land Management Socorro Field Office.

—Marti Niman

Calmed by Nature

I must admit, when I embark on the Quebradas Back Country Byway, I feel a little apprehension. To calm me down before traveling solo along this route that is definitely off the beaten path, I start my tour from the south—at the Bosque del Apache National Wildlife Refuge.

Always, when I'm in the area in winter, I plan to watch either the "fly-out" at dawn, when the birds leave the lakes en masse for the surrounding grain fields, or the "fly-in" at sunset, when they return. Though the Bosque del Apache is home to some 377 bird species, the real draw to this 57,331-acre refuge is the sheer number of them. In winter, the Bosque del Apache may harbor 45,000 snow geese, 57,000 ducks of many species and 18,000 sandhill cranes.

An ocotillo plant graces the landscape along the Quebradas Back Country Byway.

I arrive at dawn as the sun burns red on the horizon, while uncountable numbers of cranes and geese dwell on the water. One bird lifts up, then another. Their great wings flap and their caws vibrate around me, while suddenly all the birds seem to leap in one giant cloud into the air.

I stand mesmerized, my heart calmed by their beauty and ready to embark on the Quebradas Back Country Byway. But as I turn onto the dirt road, my pulse speeds up again. At first I think it is my apprehension returning, but then I realize it's the beauty that excites me. This is a place with no fences, no power lines, nothing but nature's glory.

Prickly pear cactus along the dirt road bears bright pink fruit and the land's colors appear like a pastel artist's palette: scarlet, ochre and green against a perfect sapphire sky.

I pull out my camera. Rare is the time I get to simply *play* with it, to shoot abstractly, but this, with all the varied shapes, is a photographer's paradise. I'm mesmerized by an ocotillo forest, its sprawling arms reaching to the sky, and by a *quebrada*, or break, in the hillside that offers views of mountains hundreds of miles to the west.

Suddenly, a roadrunner, my favorite bird and New Mexico's state bird as well, darts out in front of my car. I slow down as he runs along, leading me through the last section of road, his tail feathers twitching as he sprints. I realize that my heart is completely settled, any trepidation eclipsed by the beauty that has welcomed me.

Opposite, inset: The Gila Cliff Dwellings National Monument is one of the highlights of the Trail of the Mountain Spirits National Scenic Byway.

Photo by James Orr

TRAIL OF THE MOUNTAIN SPIRITS . . .

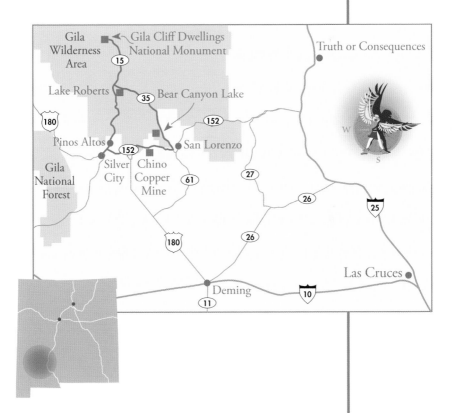

The 93-mile Trail of the Mountain Spirits National Scenic Byway beckons you to experience the beauties of southwestern New Mexico.

Walk where the spirits of all the people—miners, homesteaders, Indians, Spanish explorers, mountain men—who have passed through this area left their mark. And, like those who came before, the beauty of the surroundings will leave its mark on you.

Start in San Lorenzo, at the junction of state roads N.M. 152 and N.M. 35, in the Mimbres Valley. San Lorenzo is a quiet village, but on the feast day of its namesake, pilgrims have been known to come from as far away as California to walk, sometimes barefoot, to the small miracle room at the historic San Lorenzo Church. Plaster statues of religious figures gaze benignly from all around the room. The intense warmth seems to emanate from their eyes as well as the many burning candles.

Drive on west down N.M. 35 through the Mimbres Valley. Watch for the cutoff to Bear Canyon Lake, a little jewel offering fishing and recreation. On the lake road, look off to your left at a view that captures the essence of the Mimbres Valley: Horses graze peacefully in lush, irrigated fields. It's easy to see why this valley has been a desirable place to live for thousands of years.

A little farther west, you will see a sign marking the Continental Divide National Scenic Trail, a primitive hiking trail. The loop made by the Trail of the Mountain Spirits crosses the Continental Divide Trail twice, accessing a 14-mile-long segment through forested country that offers a visual feast of butterflies, birds and wildflowers. Combine hiking and birding on a new trail created by the New Mexico Audubon Council. At eight desig-

Opposite: The Gila Wilderness Area offers miles of hiking trails and scenic vistas.

Photo by James Orr

nated stops along the byway, you can look for some of the 337 species of birds that frequent the area.

Continue west to Lake Roberts, an oasis for the creatures of the wilderness. It's common to see herds of deer grazing along the road near the lake. Past the lake, turn right on N.M. 15. Nineteen miles on a mountain road take you to Gila Cliff Dwellings National Monument. Although small when compared with Bandelier National Monument or Mesa Verde National Park, it doesn't suffer in comparison. The beauty of the setting and the few visitors you will encounter make this destination well worth the drive.

Head back south down N.M. 15 to the old mining community of Pinos Altos. Gold was discovered here in 1860, and many of the buildings from that era are still standing. On summer weekend evenings, you can catch a melodrama at the Pinos Altos Opera House such as "Dumb Guns, or I Got Brains that Jingle, Jangle, Jingle" and take in the local color at the Buckhorn Saloon.

Continue south on N.M. 15, east on U.S. 180, then northeast on N.M. 152. An overlook on N.M. 152 reveals a panoramic view of the Chino mine, one of the largest open pit copper mines in the world. Trucks bigger than houses look like mechanical ants. The Kneeling Nun, a landmark geological formation and the source of many local legends, overlooks the mine. A few more miles bring you back to your starting point at San Lorenzo.

—Laurie Evans Frantz

Opposite: Lake Roberts provides a wonderful oasis for wildlife.

Photo: Dan Monaghan, N.M. Tourism Department

Hummingbird Heaven

I n the village of Lake Roberts along the Trail of the Mountain Spirits, a wildlife specialist gently holds a hummingbird up to my ear. The tiny creature stays completely still, its heartbeat like rushing water. Then, gently, the specialist sets it on my palm, where I can barely feel its weight. It sits still for moments, long enough for me to consider what makes this bird so fascinating.

It flies not only forward but also straight up and down, sideways, and backward, beating its wings some 50 times per second and traveling up to 35 miles per hour. It weighs as little as a penny and yet is strong enough to fly all the way from here to Alaska.

Best of all, in Lake Roberts during the summer, the striking, iridescent birds are everywhere.

In this village named for a pine-surrounded lake, every home and business caters to the tiny zoomers. The few restaurants here have picture windows looking out on multiple feeders. While eating, diners can watch the birds through glass as their little throats swallow and wings flap so fast they're invisible.

Many believe Lake Roberts is blessed with birds because of the atti-

tude here: People appreciate and protect them. And it's not just nine varieties of hummingbirds that frequent the area. Bald eagles, sapsuckers, Montezuma quail, osprey and the rarer purple martin pass through, to name only a few of the species.

Besides having such a welcoming attitude toward birds, Lake Roberts has an ideal location to attract them. It sits within the 3.3 million-acre Gila National Forest, and is on a migratory route directed by the Rocky Mountains. All the flowing water of the Gila and Mimbres rivers provides a rich habitat as well.

Here the hummingbird sits on my palm, so light I can only sense it, so fragile that I don't even want to think of all the ways it could be harmed. These unique creatures possess an equal balance of the coveted qualities—delicacy and strength. In a rush of feathers, it zooms away. I ball my palm to hold the memory near.

Opposite: Joan Day Martin gently holds a hummingbird at the Hummingbirds of New Mexico Festival in Lake Roberts.

GERONIMO TRAIL . . .

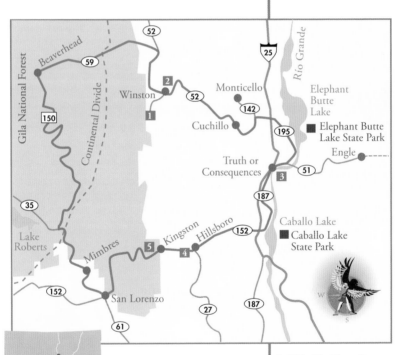

1. Chloride Ghost Town
2. Winston Historical District
3. Geronimo Springs Museum
4. Hillsboro Historical District
5. Emory Pass Vista

"I was born on the prairies where the wind blew free and there was nothing to break the light of the sun. I was born where there were no enclosures..." Geronimo

From the creosote- and cholla-swept sands of the Chiricahua Desert to the piñon and ponderosa cliffs of the Gila Wilderness, the wild freedom expressed by Chiricahua Apache warrior Geronimo more than a century ago embodies the scenic byway named in his honor. Born in a quirky desert town built over bubbling underground hot springs, the Geronimo Trail Scenic Byway taps the largest reservoir in New Mexico before twisting its way to the nation's first declared wilderness. En route are rugged carved canyons, thickly wooded mountain passes, quaint villages and ghost towns that still number a few live souls in their ledgers.

In the town of Truth or Consequences (T or C), the Geronimo Trail Visitors Center and Geronimo Springs Museum offer information and exhibits on Geronimo and local history, from mastodons to the memorabilia of Ralph Edwards, the TV host whose 1950s-era game show gave the town its name. The road loops past bright pastel-painted shops to the dune-colored beaches of 43-mile-long Elephant Butte Lake. With 200 miles of shoreline, three marinas, a visitor center, boating, water skiing, fishing and camping, Elephant Butte Lake State Park is a watery mecca for drought-parched desert denizens. On Memorial Day weekend, its population sometimes spikes to 100,000 revelers. The reservoir's dam was completed in 1916 by the U.S. Bureau of Reclamation to impound Río Grande waters for irrigation,

Opposite, inset: Kids enjoy having fun in the sun at Elephant Butte Lake State Park.

Photo courtesy of N.M. State Parks

Travelers with a good imagination can see how the land formation in the lake inspired the naming of Elephant Butte Lake State Park.

Photo by Mike Stauffer, N.M. Tourism Department

Opposite: Craig Dan Goseyun's sculpture of an Apache dancer reminds us of the byway's namesake, Geronimo.

Photo by Steve Larese

some of which soak nearby Hatch's famous hot chile fields.

The byway's northern route leaves the "Butte" on N.M. 181 and turns toward the foothills on N.M. 52 past the ranches and pecan orchards of Cuchillo, a one-time stage stop and trading center. A side trip north up N.M. 142 coasts 10 miles through pungent creosote scrub and sculpted arroyos before dropping into a verdant valley. Winding through the vine-covered adobe walls of Monticello, a village that recalls Tuscany with its lavender fields, hand-hewn church and flower-strewn plaza, the road abruptly ends on a dirt trail at desert's door.

From Cuchillo, N.M. 52 heads to the twin "ghost towns" of Winston and Chloride, silver-mining communities dating from 1881.

The Pioneer Museum's restoration is part of its ongoing history and a tour of the one-time general store is peppered with anecdotes about the eccentric characters that once strolled its wooden floors. A 200-year-old oak "hanging tree" graces the center of Main Street but, as the folks from the Pioneer Museum will tell you, no one actually was hanged in it—although a few drunk cowboys and miners were dunked in the horse trough and tied there to sober up.

Nine miles north, the byway turns west on N.M. 59 and climbs 31 miles through the vanilla-scented ponderosa stands of the Gila National Forest to the Beaverhead Ranger Station. For those traveling in four-wheel-drive vehicles, F.R. 150 heads south along the west side of the Aldo Leopold Wilderness past Wall Lake, recently reopened to the public. Check with the Gila Forest for current road conditions before braving the ruts and gullies of this backcountry dirt road, which ends at the byway's southern section on N.M. 35. For those who opt for pavement, retrace the byway route back to Interstate 25 and head for the southern route at the Hillsboro exit on N.M. 152.

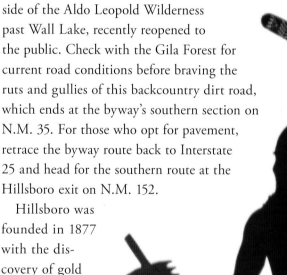

Hillsboro was founded in 1877 with the discovery of gold in the Mimbres Mountains. Now a budding retirement area of about 160 citizens, the town offers restaurants, gift shops, galleries and a museum. Farther west is the one-time wild Western town of Kingston, which in 1882 boasted one church, 22 saloons, a brewery, three newspapers, a theater and a brothel located on Virtue Street.

The byway hairpins west up to Emory Pass in the Black Range, offering panoramas of deep forest green set against rolling desert sands beyond. Dropping downhill, the road enters San Lorenzo, a village founded in 1714, now a ranching community spread along the banks of the Mimbres River. The byway continues north on N.M. 35 along the river to meet F.R. 150 in the Gila National Forest. Travelers may connect here to the Trail of the Mountain Spirits National Scenic Byway or retrace their steps to I-25, where a short jaunt south leads to Caballo Lake State Park.

A smaller version of its elephantine cousin farther north, Caballo Lake is a resting area for numerous migrating bald and golden eagles from October through the spring months. At the park's gateway is a cactus garden with pathways among huge flowering yuccas, century plants, ocotillo, cow's tongue and prickly pear. Like the Butte, Caballo Lake is a favorite warm-water fishing spot for bass, walleye, crappie, bluegill, northern pike and sunfish.

Travelers may test their eyes and ears on some of the best birding opportunities in the state, both in the lower elevation riparian areas and the wooded Gila country. A free southwestern New Mexico birding map, as well as a statewide fishing map, are available from the New Mexico Department of Game and Fish. Road-weary travelers may return to T or C for a bone-melting soak in one of its many hot springs and revel in the sunlight and freedom this wild southern country has to offer.

—Marti Niman

Winston was once a booming mining town. Today it is a quieter town that celebrates its mining history.

Photo by Mark Nohl

Ghost Town Shopping

M y name is Lesley King, and I am "shopping challenged." Over the years, I've come to accept it, and now my life is easier. When I step into a mall, my skin grows icy and my sight blurry. Too much stuff, too many decisions to make. But I must say, I really enjoy shopping along the Geronimo Trail National Scenic Byway. Maybe it's the simplicity that helps me let down my guard. Or maybe it's the fact that I'm shopping in ghost towns.

My first stop is Chloride, where I eat a sandwich at their lovely picnic area and tour the Pioneer Museum. Then I head next door to

a little shop filled with art made by creative people who have sought solitude in these remote hills. I find a bright cross-pendant made by a woman in nearby Dusty and a dragonfly sculpture by a man from Chloride itself.

As I drive to my next stop, I snack on my last purchase, some delicious green-chile pecans and buffalo jerky. At the general store in Winston, a cloth handbag adorned with chile peppers crafted by an artist just up the road will make a great gift for my mom, and some local jewelry made with elk ivory just might appeal to my niece.

My ultimate ghost town shopping spot is Hillsboro. Here, I encounter galleries filled with photographs and paintings that depict the region's grassy hills and quaint buildings. I also find gourd bowls decorated with whimsical horses and earthy tables made from native woods.

Most of the works are quality art, crafted with care by people who choose to live close to nature. In my travels I've met some of them—a painter and a photographer in Hillsboro, for example—people who are inspired to re-create the beauty around them. The prices help ease my shopping anxiety, but more than that, I find something personal in these purchases, a connection to the place and time that I'll remember whenever I gaze upon the artwork or hold it in my hand.

Opposite: Cheryl Aber, who lives in the nearby town of Dusty, created the cross pendant.

Below: Artist Doug Lyons, of the Chloride area, crafted the dragonfly sculpture from a wrench.

Or maybe, I'll arrive home with an opaque wisp that dissolves into nothing—after all these *are* ghost towns.

LAKE VALLEY BACK COUNTRY . . .

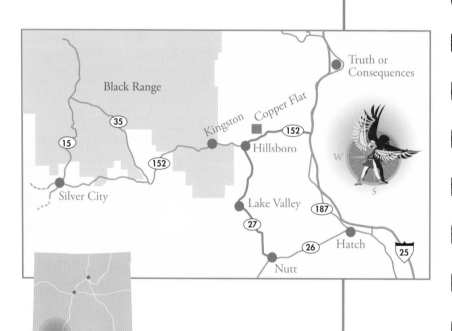

Truth or Consequences

Black Range

Kingston   Copper Flat

35

15

152

Hillsboro

152

Silver City

Lake Valley

27

187

26   Hatch

Nutt

25

California is known for its gold rush, but New Mexico also had its mining fever. Lake Valley Back Country Scenic Byway delves deep into the heart of the mineral-rich Black Range Mountains.

To explore the territory, turn off I-25 south of Truth or Consequences onto N.M. 152 and head for Hillsboro.

The history of mining in the Black Range spans a period of more than 100 years. Silver was discovered along the banks of Percha Creek, near the present town of Kingston, in 1877. The rush was on, and prospectors scoured the hills for precious minerals. They found silver south of Hillsboro in 1878, and with the discovery of the spectacular Bridal Chamber claim in 1882, the Black Range was the place to be.

Silver and gold are still mined on a small scale, but the largest mining operation in recent years is at Copper Flat. On the way to Hillsboro, look for the Bureau of Land Management kiosk on the south side of the road. It points out the open-pit copper mine, earthen dam and water towers built in 1982, which aided in the extraction of 7.4 million pounds of copper, 2,306 ounces of gold and 55,966 ounces of silver in a three-month period.

The observant traveler can see evidence of smaller-scale mining operations along the byway. The scars of exploratory excavations into hillsides and the cascade of multicolored waste rock below are sure signs of past mining activities. Along the arroyo just east of milepost 54 are mounds of dirt, the remains of gold panning.

As N.M. 152 winds west into the Black Range, the terrain gets hillier. Hillsboro, a village of 165 people, is

Opposite, inset: Hillsboro is a charming, historic mining town.

Photo by Dan Monaghan, N.M. Tourism Department

nestled in the foothills along Percha Creek. A drive through its shady, tree-lined streets reveals many buildings from the late 1800s. The 1892 Union Church stands next door to the George and Ninette Miller House, built in 1894. The ruins of a jail and courthouse are relics of the period from 1884 to 1939 when Hillsboro was the Sierra County seat.

The 1879 Miller Drug Store has been a mercantile, pharmacy, grocery, post office and telephone exchange and is now a café. The Black Range Museum (open by appointment) was once the Ocean Grove Hotel, run by Sadie Orchard, a well-known local character who made her living as a madam, hotel owner and stagecoach operator. The proprietor of the clock shop down the street will tell you he can't remember how long he's been here: You lose track of time in Hillsboro.

The byway turns south on N.M. 27, headed for Lake Valley. Along the road, there is a large stand of ocotillo, one of the high desert's most interesting plants. The skinny, spiny fingers stand tall against the horizon, woody branches creaking as they wave in the wind.

In the 1880s, travel through this area was very dangerous due to attacks by bandits and Apaches. Sadie Orchard's stagecoach would meet passengers at the train in Lake Valley and take them to Hillsboro, sometimes with Sadie at the reins.

Many so-called ghost towns in New Mexico are actually now repopulated, but Lake Valley is the real thing. Its last residents moved to Deming in 1994. It is now partially owned by the Bureau of Land Management, which offers a free self-guided walking tour. The schoolhouse museum is the place to start; Lake Valley artifacts are displayed inside.

In 1882, the richest single body of silver ever found, 10 to 20 feet thick, was discovered nearby, and miners flocked to Lake Valley. The claim was named the Bridal Chamber because light reflecting off the crystal-encrusted walls dazzled the miners' eyes. The ore was so pure

Take a walking tour through the authentic ghost town of Lake Valley.

Photo by Dan Monaghan, N.M. Tourism Department

it was reportedly sawed off in blocks rather than blasted. This mine produced 2.5 million ounces of silver during the next 12 years. But when the demand for silver declined, so did the town. The value of silver dropped dramatically when it was demonetized in 1893. The flimsy miners' homes didn't last long after their occupants moved on, and a fire that destroyed Main Street in June 1895 further desolated the town.

The old ghost town still has its pleasures. As you walk, listen to the whispering of the tall grass, the conversations of insects and birds, and the staccato beat of loose sheet metal flapping in the wind. The clean smell of greasewood sweetens the air. Large black bees—like airborne Volkswagens—gather pollen, while surprised lizards scurry for cover.

The byway continues east to Nutt, paralleling a spur line of the Atchison, Topeka and Santa Fe Railway, built in 1884 to transport supplies in to Lake Valley and ore out. In 1934, the tracks were removed, but the grade is still visible. The remains of a loading ramp can be seen at Nutt, where the byway ends. The ramp leads to nothing now, but those tracks once carried a prodigious load of wealth and people whose lives intersected on what is now the Lake Valley Back Country Scenic Byway.

—Laurie Evans Frantz

Opposite: Mining equipment from Lake Valley.
Photo by Lesley S. King

The Promise of a Ghost Town

E ver since high school, when I first started taking photographs, I've loved wandering through ghost towns—places that once bustled with life but are now empty and creaky, full of broken glass, tarnished metal and aged wood.

For a photographer, such images are pure gold, but on my trip along the Lake Valley Scenic Byway, I realize there's a deeper reason for my love of wandering through forgotten places.

I stop at Lake Valley itself and start my tour at the schoolhouse, which operated from 1904 to 1941. The big adobe building holds a blackboard and wooden desks, along with memorabilia from the mining days—iron tools and antique books. Most notable though is a survey map showing the many mining claims on this land in 1881, the height of this town's production.

When I head out onto the streets, my interest piques. Even though much of Lake Valley burned in an 1895 fire, it still has a feel of a *real* town, with buildings set along a street, where once oxen "bull trains" pulled wagons through.

Today, the clear New Mexico light sparkles as it hits glass panes, rusted pulleys and eroded adobe walls. I stop to read one of the plaques that tells the town's story. It explains that in the year 1895,

the Keller-Miller Store sold today's equivalent of $1 million worth of flour, tobacco, coffee, spirits, clothing and shoes.

Now, all that bustle is quiet except for the grass rustling in the breeze and a bluejay flitting by. It's amazing that something so massive as a whole town would be reduced to this. It's comforting for me, as I move through life, leaving old jobs and relationships and starting new ones, life constantly changing—the old dying to make way for the bounty of the new.

Above: The wind whistles through abandoned buildings in Lake Valley.

Opposite, inset: Tales persist about notorious outlaw William H. Bonney, aka Billy the Kid.

BILLY THE KID . . .

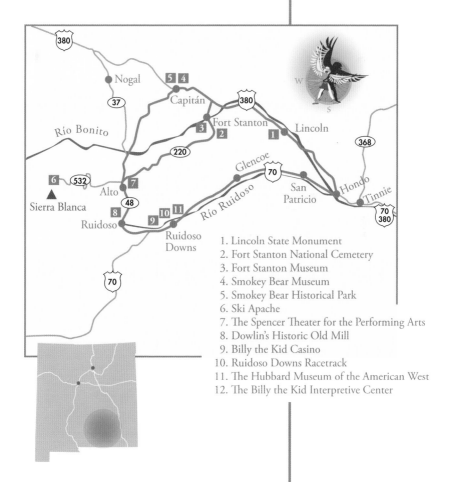

1. Lincoln State Monument
2. Fort Stanton National Cemetery
3. Fort Stanton Museum
4. Smokey Bear Museum
5. Smokey Bear Historical Park
6. Ski Apache
7. The Spencer Theater for the Performing Arts
8. Dowlin's Historic Old Mill
9. Billy the Kid Casino
10. Ruidoso Downs Racetrack
11. The Hubbard Museum of the American West
12. The Billy the Kid Interpretive Center

The Wild West lore of gunfights, horses, outlaws, Buffalo Soldiers and Smokey Bear comes to life along the Billy the Kid National Scenic Byway, where legends play against a spectacular backdrop of snowy peaks, rolling rivers, orchards and ranchlands.

From the one-horse, one-street town of Lincoln, where Billy the Kid and Pat Garrett sparred to the bustling ski-town ruckus of Ruidoso, the byway offers a legendary West both present and past.

At the Billy the Kid Interpretive Center in Ruidoso Downs, kids of all ages may straddle a virtual map painted on the gallery floor, complete with 3-D mountains. Next door, the Hubbard Museum of the American West boasts buggies, stagecoaches, antique firearms, Plains Indian beadwork and Pueblo *katsinas* inside its walls, while outside a herd of life-size bronze horses representing major American breeds gallops through the garden. Ruidoso Downs Racetrack, open Memorial Day through Labor Day, is home to the world's richest quarter-horse race, the All American Futurity, offering a guaranteed $1 million purse to the winner.

The trail turns north on N.M. 48 through rustic Ruidoso, Spanish for "noisy"—a reference to the boisterous water rushing in the river along its main drag. Snowy Sierra Blanca, at 12,003 feet elevation, soars above the false-front stores, shops and restaurants clustered in the village below. Dowlin's Historic Old Mill is remarkable for its still-functioning water mill and notorious because it once hid outlaw Billy the Kid. Continuing to tiny Alto, travelers may head west to the white-flanked slopes of Ski Apache on N.M. 532—a road so narrow and knotted that uphill traffic is banned

Opposite: Majestic Sierra Blanca soars 12,003 feet above the town of Ruidoso.

Photo by Steve Larese

Fort Stanton was established by the U.S. Infantry in 1855.

Photo by Mike Stauffer, N.M. Tourism Department

between 3 to 6 p.m. during ski season. The resort is owned by the Mescalero Apaches, descendants of bands whose resistance to unwelcome settlers in their homeland prompted the U.S. Infantry to establish nearby Fort Stanton in 1855.

Those of a more artistic than athletic bent may head east on N.M. 220 to the sparkling white slab of the Spencer Theater for the Performing Arts. In its cloud-like setting, the crystal and limestone monolith could be a spaceship sidetracked from Roswell rather than a state-of-the-art performance stage. It offers world-class productions year-round and glass sculptures by renowned artist Dale Chihuly on permanent exhibit.

N.M. 220 cuts across the top of the world through a piñon-juniper woodland, offering circular views of windswept peaks before dropping into the Río Bonito Valley. Here, the monument and white crosses of Fort Stanton National Cemetery mark the land-locked final resting place

Billy the Kid worked as a hand at the Coe Ranch, in Glencoe.

Photo by Mike Stauffer, N.M. Tourism Department

of merchant marines far inland from their ocean realm. The marines were treated for tuberculosis at Fort Stanton, a few miles up the road, which metamorphosed through the years from a military post, to a hospital, internment camp, jail and halfway house for youth. A number of notable and notorious individuals strolled its hallways at one time: Kit Carson; "Black Jack" Pershing; the 9th Cavalry of the Buffalo Soldiers—so named by the Apaches because their wooly hair and fighting spirit reminded them of buffalo; and one William H. Bonney, aka Billy the Kid. Fort Stanton Museum provides guided tours and information. Special events such as military re-enactments and horse riding events are presented throughout the year.

At U.S. 380, travelers may head west toward Capitán, home of Smokey Bear, or east toward Lincoln. Smokey, the tiny cub, was

The Lincoln County Jail, made famous by Billy the Kid's daring escape in 1881.

Photo by Dan Monaghan, N.M. Tourism Department

Opposite: Billy the Kid's memory lives on in Lincoln and other towns along the Billy the Kid National Scenic Byway.

discovered clinging to a tree during a human-caused forest fire that raged through Capitán Gap in 1950. The cub, initially nicknamed "Hotfoot" for his badly burned feet and buttocks, was flown to a Santa Fe veterinary hospital by Department of Game and Fish officer Ray Bell. Eventually the bear lived at the National Zoo in Washington, D.C., until his death in 1976, when his remains were returned for burial in Capitán. The Smokey Bear Museum and Smokey Bear Historical Park, in Capitán, display the story of Smokey Bear and firefighters of the West.

U.S. 380 heads east through Lincoln, a town whose tranquil lone street belies its unruly past as the stage for one of the last great gunfights in the Old West. The Lincoln County War erupted between warring mercantile factions after a young Englishman, John Tunstall, challenged the monopoly of the J. J. Dolan and Company general store in 1877. Tunstall was murdered within the year and Billy the Kid, a former Tunstall ranch hand, swore to avenge Tunstall's death. The conflicting stories of Billy the Kid play out in the town landmarks, many of which are preserved to the last brick and shutter as part of Lincoln State Monument.

Continuing eastward, U.S. 380 follows the Río Bonito and the lush rural orchards and ranches of the Hondo Valley, where it joins the Río Ruidoso at U.S. 70 near Hondo. The orchards burst into bloom in springtime and are radiant in fall with gold and yellow leaves. The late sculptor Luis Jiménez made his studio and workshop in Hondo, while in San Patricio the Hurd-Rinconada Gallery exhibits the paintings of Michael Hurd, as well as the work of one-time residents Henrietta Wyeth and Peter Hurd. U.S. 70 finally returns to Ruidoso Downs, where visitors may try their hand at virtual video blackjack or play the slots at Billy the Kid Casino for a last nostalgic take on the Old West before heading home.

—Marti Niman

Friends along the Way

A primary stop along the Billy the Kid Scenic Byway ranks as my favorite village in New Mexico: Lincoln. It is one of the best-preserved 19th-century towns in the U.S., without a single neon sign or fast-food anything, its streets lined with adobe buildings that have been tended and renovated by a handful of people who appreciate the region.

The night I truly fell in love with the town I was staying in one of its historic bed and breakfasts and decided to take a walk. Immediately I noted a skunk about 10 paces behind me. Slightly alarmed, I picked up my pace.

He did, too.

The town was quiet, as always at night, with a sickle moon in the sky and yellow lights glowing from a few windows. I walked the full length of Lincoln, past the Anderson-Freeman Visitor Center, where portraits of all the players in the Lincoln County War line the walls, and by the Tunstall Store, which was a focal point of the war.

At the Old Lincoln County Courthouse, from which Billy the Kid escaped, I crossed the street and walked back. The skunk followed me the whole way.

For me, this byway is about sweet encounters like that.

Along its route I once met a jewelry maker in Hondo who invited me into her studio to watch her work. In San Patricio I struck up a conversation with artist Michael Hurd, son of the noted Peter Hurd, who described his efforts to preserve the Río Ruidoso running through his property. And in Capitán, an elderly couple invited me into the museum they had created by collecting a lifetime of antiques.

Such encounters are common here because a small-town attitude prevails, with trust as the main ingredient. So when I take this loop, I slip on my walking shoes and open my heart. I just may be lucky enough to meet a valuable (if slightly stinky) new friend.

Opposite and below: A mural at Lincoln's Anderson-Freeman Visitors Center depicts Billy the Kid's role in the shootout during the Lincoln County War.

SUNSPOT . . .

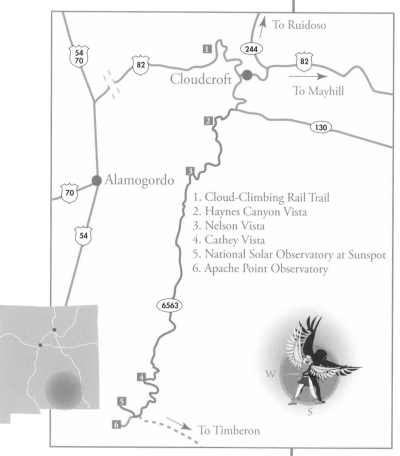

To Ruidoso

54
70

82

244

82

Cloudcroft

To Mayhill

130

Alamogordo

70

3

54

1. Cloud-Climbing Rail Trail
2. Haynes Canyon Vista
3. Nelson Vista
4. Cathey Vista
5. National Solar Observatory at Sunspot
6. Apache Point Observatory

6563

4

5

6

To Timberon

W

S

The "faraway nearby" is close at hand on the Sunspot Scenic Byway, a short sweet sprig of asphalt through deep, dark woodlands offering occasional peeks at dunes, deserts and sprawling mountains beyond.

Earthshaking as these vistas are, the Sunspot Scenic Byway's sphere of views doesn't stop at the mere horizon but expands to galaxies, nebulae and solar systems of the final frontier. Two national telescope observatories at the byway's terminus offer tours and exhibits to the earthbound public, while a consortium of scientists explores the heavens from its 9,200-foot elevation.

The 15-mile road begins two miles south of Cloudcroft, off N.M. 130, where the Cloudcroft Ranger District of the Lincoln National Forest provides maps and information. The town of Cloudcroft is named for the puffy clouds that frequently hug its forested hillsides. The byway officially is designated N.M. 6563—the light wavelength in angstroms used by scientists to locate active areas on the sun.

At Haynes Canyon Vista, mere mortals may locate distant Earth landmarks like Hardscrabble and Little Burro mountains, Oscura and San Andres peaks, and the shimmering radiance of White Sands. As the road zigzags along the front rim of the Sacramento Mountains, through pine, aspen and fir forests, similar lookouts provide a glimpse at the dramatic scenery some 5,000 feet below as well as access to numerous hiking trails. The 13.5-mile Rim Trail, a National Recreation Trail, parallels a portion of the byway with spectacular views of the Tularosa Basin some 5,000 feet below.

Opposite, inset: The Lodge Resort in Cloudcroft welcomes visitors with meals and accommodations.

Photo by Mike Stauffer, N.M. Tourism Department

Surrounded by mountains, the Tularosa Basin encompasses 275 square miles of crystal white-sand waves that lap up everything in their path as they are driven relentlessly by southwesterly winds. This ocean of sand, White Sands, was born in a shallow sea that covered the area 250 million years ago. Gypsum deposited beneath the sea turned to stone and shattered into sand crystals from the force of headlong winds. The dunes of White Sands are an immense, luminous mirage as seen from the heady heights of the Sunspot Byway and are home to both a missile range and a national monument.

On clear days, one may glimpse Spaceport America. Traveling backward in time, an old railroad grade from the 1900s parallels sections of the Sunspot Byway and some remnant wooden trestles may be visible. The Bluff Springs Trail offers an easy hike along abandoned grades of the old Cloudcroft logging railroad.

Back to the future at the end of the Sunspot Byway, the Sunspot Visitor Center and Museum first opened in July 1997 as a collaboration between the National Solar Observatory/Sacramento Peak, Apache Point Observatory, the National Scenic Byways program, and the U.S. Forest Service. Sacramento Peak boasts some of the darkest, clearest skies in the country—at the opposite end of the road and climatic spectrum from misty Cloudcroft. Outside the museum's interactive exhibits, visitors are greeted by the Armillary Sphere and Sundial, a 5-foot diameter bronze sculpture showing the relationship between earth and sky in Sunspot.

The glistening gypsum dunes at White Sands National Monument delight travelers of all ages.

Photo by James Orr

At Apache Point Observatory, access to the telescopes and buildings is restricted but visitors are welcome to stroll the grounds. The desert skies of the Sacramento Mountains offer low humidity, low dust and very dark,

transparent skies for observing the galaxies and nebulae of deep space. Scientists operate these telescopes by remote control via the Internet from aircraft, satellite links and even the South Pole. The National Solar Observatory telescopes are designed for sun watchers.

The Vacuum Tower contains a 329-foot-long tube with the air removed, so images of the sun won't shimmer the way White Sands does. The visible tower soars 136 feet overhead but most of the structure dives 228 feet below ground.

The Big Dome holds two main telescopes: One allows astronomers to study the sun's corona by creating an artificial eclipse with a disk blocking the brilliant sun; the other observes transient solar events like flares that eject particles that can reach Earth, causing the Aurora Borealis and disrupting some radio communications. Stars are made up mostly of the hydrogen wavelength of 6,563 angstroms. Using this wavelength, scientists may observe the sun's atmosphere at cloud level and see clouds as well as sunspots, which one solar observer claims to resemble little black dots or eye pupils—complete with eyelashes.

Rumor has it the observatory ordered a grain bin from a Sears catalog back in 1950, when it was the first telescope dome built in Sunspot. Sunspot residents now use the Grain Bin Dome at night to watch the stars and moon.

Byway visitors may continue on the mostly-paved highway to the small ranching community of Timberon, or head back to Cloudcroft to continue space exploration at the New Mexico Museum of Space History in Alamogordo. En route, visit two of 58 wooden railroad trestles dating from the mid-19th century on the Cloud Climbing Rail Trail off U.S. 82.

Above: The wooden railroad trestles are highlights on the Cloud Climbing Rail Trail.

Photo by Mike Stauffer, N.M. Tourism Department

Opposite: One of the rockets on display outside of the New Mexico Museum of Space History.

Photo by Steve Larese

Cloudcroft once could be reached only by a locomotive that hauled passengers and freight 6,000 scary feet up a precipitous canyon. The remnant S curve trestles spanning the canyon are an impressive link in our perpetual human quest to bring the faraway nearby.

—Marti Niman

Finding a New Pace in Cloudcroft

S ometimes my mother hauls me away from my bustling life and takes me down to Cloudcroft, just off the Sunspot Scenic Byway. Since both of us enjoy elegant historic hotels such as The Plaza in New York and the Broadmoor in Colorado Springs, we like the Old World feel of The Lodge Resort in Cloudcroft, as well as the town itself, which reflects the Western spirit and relaxed pace of long ago. At first I can struggle with that pace, as I do on this trip, my mother shaking her head as she basks in relaxation.

The Lodge Resort in Cloudcroft beckons visitors.

The Lodge arose for just such a purpose. In the late 1800s, the El Paso and Northeastern Railroad ran a train track up into these mountains to haul away trestle timber. They built a grand Victorian hotel, which later burned, but in 1911 was replaced by this one, with a five-story tower, plush velvet interior, and views out across the cloudlike White Sands National Monument some 4,500 feet below. Visitors would come to enjoy the cool mountain air.

After a good night sleep, we head over to Burro Street and get a sense of Cloudcroft. It has an Old West feel, the buildings adorned with wooden storefronts and filled with shops and cafes, which we wander through aimlessly. One of the highest towns in the state, Cloudcroft sits at 8,650 feet and has about 750 inhabitants, though that number triples in summer. The town grew up as a vacation village around The Lodge, but many visitors have come to stay. Says one of them: "You won't see too many clocks here. Nobody cares about time." I must say, I am checking my watch only a few times an hour now.

While shopping we find locally crafted pottery, paintings of southern New Mexico landscapes, and some funky hand-stitched clothing. Then we tour the Sacramento Mountains Historical Museum and Pioneer Village. In the museum, we get a deeper sense of the area's history, beginning with habitation by the Mescalero Apaches, who still live here. We find Apache arrowheads and pottery, models of the "impossible" railroad, and dazzling period photos of the town's younger days. In the Pioneer Village we learn about early farming and ranching through century-old artifacts and an authentic log cabin. It's almost enough to lure this racing-about-the-world travel writer into a simpler, slower existence.

GUADALUPE BACK COUNTRY . . .

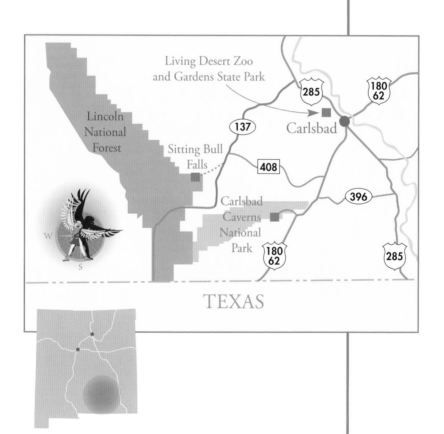

Living Desert Zoo
and Gardens State Park

285

180
62

137

Carlsbad

Lincoln
National
Forest

Sitting Bull
Falls

408

396

Carlsbad
Caverns
National
Park

180
62

285

W

S

TEXAS

The story of the Guadalupe Back Country Scenic Byway (N.M. 137) is told by the odors you encounter along the route—odors that entice you, assail you and even assault you at times.

These scents are clues to the natural beauty of the region itself and the industries that sustain its people.

The first thing you may smell is creosote bush. It freshens the air like recent rain and reminds you that you're driving through southern New Mexico's ranch country. Sooner or later a less pleasant odor heralds your entry into oil and gas territory. Sometimes this smell can be dangerous—if you encounter hydrogen sulfide gas, for instance. At Sitting Bull Falls, water flowing over desert rocks emits a sweet smell, and the breeze carries a faint scent reminiscent of licorice.

The 30 miles of the byway run through land managed by the Bureau of Land Management. A kiosk at the beginning of the route states the bureau's purpose: "striking a balance on public lands." The balance is between public use and protection of recreation, private land use and management of natural resources along N.M. 137.

The byway begins at U.S. 285 12 miles north of Carlsbad in the Chihuahuan Desert and ascends about 3,000 feet into the Guadalupe Mountains. The terrain gets rugged quickly. Large patches of prickly pear and sotol grow out of cream-colored limestone outcrops. The desert landscape, striking as it is, conceals beauty and riches perhaps unsuspected by its earliest Paleo-Indian inhabitants 10,000 years ago.

Hidden beneath the surface are wild caves of exquisite splendor that

Opposite, inset: Flowers on the cholla cactus brighten the landscape.

Photo by Mike Stauffer, N.M. Tourism Department

draw scientists and spelunkers from all over the world. A permit to explore the caves can be obtained from the Guadalupe Ranger District, Lincoln National Forest. Seven to 12,000 feet farther below the surface are the oil and natural gas reserves of the Permian Basin, one of the largest oil and gas provinces in the United States.

Oil was first discovered in southeastern New Mexico 30 miles south of Carlsbad in 1901. The drillers were actually looking for water but hit oil at only 80 feet. The first oil well along the byway was drilled in 1917. Today, more than 28,000 wells produce oil and gas in the region.

For those with a yen for the mysteries of side roads, this byway is full of opportunities. Both improved and primitive roads intersect it along the way and lead to public lands, where you may stop for hiking, mountain biking, caving or just exploring.

Driving south on the byway, you will encounter a sign that directs you to Sitting Bull Falls Recreation Area, open year-round. The road descends eight miles through winding canyons on the way to the falls. The recreation area is for day use only; stone picnic shelters with grills are available. A paved path leads from the picnic shelters to the falls.

Two hundred million years ago, during the Permian Period, this area was an inland sea. Sitting Bull Falls is a small remnant of the waters from this ancient time. Water flowing from a spring located in the canyon above created the falls. From the observation point at the end of the paved path, a 200-foot-high wall of tufa looms in front of you. It extends up the canyon for three quarters of a mile. The formation of this lightweight, porous rock from calcium carbonate precipitating out of the water has taken hundreds of thousands of

Opposite: Horses meander through the countryside en route to Sitting Bull Falls.

Photo by Mike Stauffer, N.M. Tourism Department

years. When plants die and fall into the water, a chemical reaction occurs that forms fossils. This process is still ongoing at the bottom of the falls.

Sitting Bull Falls is nothing like Niagara Falls; it is more like a shower. A delicate flow of water trickles and splashes 150 feet down the cliff. In the late afternoon, spray bouncing off the cliff is backlit by the unseen sun. Crystal clear water flows gently into a pool at the bottom. The bright green vegetation around the falls contrasts with the usual gray-green colors of desert plants on surrounding cliffs. A cool breeze blows fitfully through the canyon. Sixteen miles of hiking trails traverse the recreational area, varying from 1.5 to 6.6 miles in length. A dirt trail striking off from the paved path leads hikers to the top of the mesa and the source of the falls. The flow of water from this spring creates a lush ribbon of vegetation paralleled by the path. Electric blue dragonflies flit across lime green ponds created by a thick blanket of algae.

The byway continues down N.M. 137 for several more miles, until the road intersects the boundary of Lincoln National Forest. The road continues through southern New Mexico into Texas—and out of the Land of Enchantment.

—Laurie Evans Frantz

Opposite: Sitting Bull Falls offers a refreshing surprise in the desert terrain.
Photo by Mike Stauffer, N.M. Tourism Department

Springing to Life

While gazing across at Sitting Bull Falls, along the Guadalupe Back Country Byway, I delight in the miniature rainbows cast in the mist and the sound of flowing water. Next to me, a voice says, "It's not Niagara Falls, it's a little bit better."

I chuckle, as does Byron Hughes, the campground host who said it. Maybe I'm just a diehard New Mexican overly proud of my home state, but I agree with him. As well as their subtle beauty falling off a moss-covered ledge of tufa, these falls have a miraculous quality about them. Within hundreds of miles of parched Chihuahuan Desert, they spring to life seemingly out of nowhere.

Today, I'm going to the top to get a glimpse of the source.

Saying goodbye to Byron, I step along a clear path that ascends up a broad hillside. I look back at the graceful stone picnic shelters, where families enjoy lunch, and beyond at the lush cactus-studded canyon.

Along every turn in the trail I encounter yet another pillowy white yucca bloom. Continuing upward, I pass piñon trees and alligator juniper, all thriving in a place that only receives about 14 inches of rain per year.

Nearing the top of the 200-foot ascent, I step onto the tufa that surrounds the falls. Beneath my feet the ground becomes spongy, much like tundra, and within the porous rock, water seeps. I continue to climb until slowly the ground levels out and there before me stands a pool.

The water is clear and blue, surrounded by ferns. Its far edge seems to fall off into oblivion, the place where the spring becomes Sitting Bull Falls. Byron told me that many springs feed the falls, and as I look in the opposite direction, I see a ribbon of green stretching a half-mile or so across the desert.

The top of Sitting Bull Falls offers a wonderful oasis in the desert environment.

I take off my shoes and dip my bare feet in the 55-degree water. Cold rushes up my body, and I become light-headed. It's a feeling of awe as I imagine the various springs running along underground and surfacing, just in time to make this little wonder.

EL CAMINO
REAL . . .

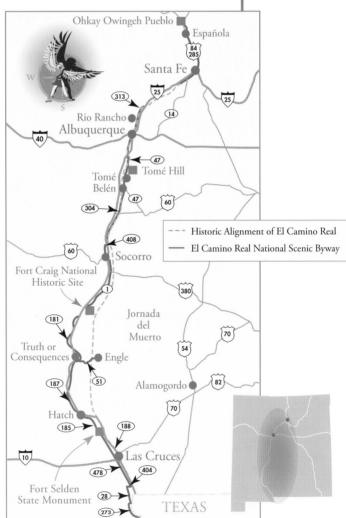

Ohkay Owingeh Pueblo

Española

84 285

Santa Fe

25

313

25

Rio Rancho

14

Albuquerque

40

47

Tomé Hill

Tomé

Belén

304

47

60

408

60

Socorro

Fort Craig National
Historic Site

1

380

181

Jornada
del
Muerto

70

Truth or
Consequences

54

Engle

187

51

Alamogordo

82

70

Hatch

185

188

10

Las Cruces

478

404

Fort Selden
State Monument

28

273

TEXAS

- - - Historic Alignment of El Camino Real
——— El Camino Real National Scenic Byway

In 1598, don Juan de Oñate led 500 colonists through remote and unfamiliar country, encountering people with vastly different languages and cultures, not knowing what awaited them at the end of the journey.

The land is now known as New Mexico, and the route Oñate followed became El Camino Real (the royal road), a trail that until then only reached the frontiers of northern Mexico. Oñate's journey was the beginning of more than four centuries of travel and commerce in New Mexico on El Camino Real, which is commemorated by a national- and state-designated scenic byway.

El Camino Real threads through New Mexico, a unifying force in the landscape and history. The city of Las Cruces (the crosses) may have been named for crosses on the graves of unfortunate travelers on El Camino Real. The Army laid out the original Las Cruces town site in 1849 in an attempt to protect local communities and travelers. The area now designated as the Mesquite Street Original Townsite Historic District is charming with its small adobe houses painted bright pink, green, and blue. Casa Colonial at the Farm and Ranch Heritage Museum represents an earlier style of Spanish architecture.

Troops were stationed at Fort Selden and at Fort Craig (35 miles south of Socorro) in the mid-1800s to protect local settlers and travelers on El Camino Real. Both forts were established near *parajes* (camps) that were first utilized by the Oñate expedition. Fort Selden is at the southern end and Fort Craig at the northern end of the Jornada del Muerto (journey of the dead man). The rough country around the Río Grande forced travelers to

Opposite, inset: Wildflowers bloom at the base of the Organ Mountains.

Photo by James Orr

Hot air balloons hover above the Río Grande in Albuquerque.

Photo by Steve Larese

cross 90 miles of flat, waterless and dangerous desert. North of Fort Selden, the byway follows the Río Grande to Truth or Consequences. The linear green oasis created by the river contrasts with the brown Caballo Mountains and Sierra de las Uvas nearby, and the faded blues of the San Andres Mountains and the Black Range on the horizon.

The interior of the San Miguel Mission in Santa Fe features thick, white-washed adobe walls.

Photo by Steve Larese

A diorama at the Geronimo Springs Museum in Truth or Consequences depicts the Jornada del Muerto, which is about 15 miles east of town on N.M. 51. A visit to this desolate area in the summer shows why early travelers moved by night and rested by day.

When Oñate reached the Piro Indian pueblo of Teypana, his group was near starvation. The Indians welcomed and fed the colonists, prompting Oñate to name the place for the Spanish word for help, Socorro. The settlement was a stop on El Camino Real until the Pueblo Revolt of 1680. The pueblo is gone, but a sculpted "Wheel of History," north of Socorro's plaza, commemorates its place in the history of the area.

Many small settlements north of Socorro that originated on El Camino Real are still inhabited today. One of these, Tomé, is the site of "La Puerta del Sol," (gateway to the sun) a monumental sculpture depicting the historic procession of travelers on El Camino Real. Tomé Hill has been a landmark for travelers since prehistoric times.

The juxtaposition of El Camino Real, a good ford on the Río Grande, and fertile farmland attracted settlers to what is now Old Town in Albuquerque in 1706. Old Town is a window into the past of New Mexico's largest metropolitan area. History comes alive at the National Hispanic Cultural Center and the Indian Pueblo Cultural Center, both located on the byway.

Agua Fria Street leads into the heart of Santa Fe, as it did when it was called El Camino Real. Sculptures in Frenchy's Field Park and Santa Fe River State Park commemorate the centuries of travel through Santa Fe on El Camino Real. The Palace of the Governors was built around 1610, when Santa Fe was established as the capital of New Mexico. It now houses a museum full of artifacts and information on New Mexico's rich history.

The byway terminates at Ohkay Owingeh Pueblo—the first capital of New Mexico and the end of don Juan de Oñate's journey. The timeless thread of El Camino Real weaves through the evolving landscape of New Mexico, connecting past and present, Río Abajo and Río Arriba. Today is just another knot in the thread of history that is El Camino Real.

—Laurie Evans Frantz

Making the Royal Road My Own

I'm like a kid—unless I can bring history into my present experience, it gives me a case of the yawns. This is not a problem while traveling the El Camino Real National Scenic Byway. Over the years, I've discovered much excitement along this journey through time.

One of my favorite stops is the El Camino Real International Heritage Center. The $5 million, 20,000-square-foot structure houses a virtual trip along the trail, with artifacts and photos from the early days of El Camino Real (the royal road). The award-winning building perches like a ship above Sheep Canyon between Socorro and Truth or Consequences.

Visitors can learn about the Spanish conquistadors' travels over the rugged desert terrain at El Camino Real International Heritage Center.

In fact, the center is designed with ship elements. "The journey across the Jornada del Muerto reminded travelers of crossing the sea, with its tufts of grass, mirages and overwhelming silence," says Monument Ranger Dave Wunker. Indeed, as I look out the many windows of the place, I have a sense of floating. The ceiling undulates, creating the sense of waves, while windows similar to portholes line one wall.

The real fun starts in the exhibition hall. Here I travel the trail, beginning at Mexico's Zacatecas Plaza, with a fountain and walls painted in warm hues. I continue up a ramp to other villages, adorned with enlarged period photos, until I reach the top story, where displays depict the Santa Fe Plaza and El Camino Real's terminus at Ohkay Owingeh Pueblo. Artifacts from the trail's early days—pottery, saddles, a *caja fuerte* (strong box) and an Apache water jug—bring the journey to life.

As I finish the trip, I really understand the magnitude of El Camino Real as a means of historic transformation. "For better or worse," writes Douglas Preston in his book *The Royal Road,* "the Camino Real changed the history of the United States and Mexico as no other trail has, before or since."

Now *that* is exciting.

Opposite, inset: Lowrider cars can often be spotted in Chimayó.

Photo by Steve Larese

HIGH ROAD TO TAOS . . .

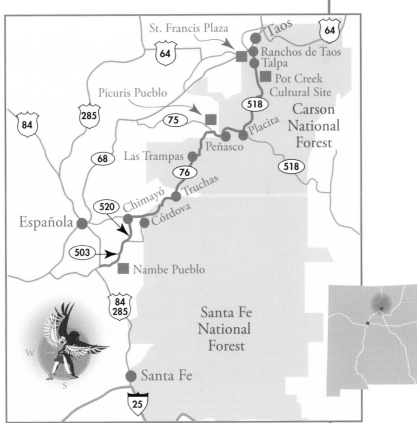

St. Francis Plaza

Taos

64

64

Ranchos de Taos
Talpa

Pot Creek
Cultural Site

Picuris Pueblo

285

75

518

Carson
National
Forest

84

Placita

68

Las Trampas

Peñasco

76

518

Chimayó

Truchas

520

Córdova

Española

503

Nambe Pueblo

84
285

Santa Fe
National
Forest

Santa Fe

25

The High Road to Taos Scenic Byway takes the traveler through an authentic remnant of Old Spain, still evident in the religion, architecture and history of the people along the route.

To begin this miraculous journey, take U.S. 84/285 north from Santa Fe and turn east on N.M. 503 to Nambe Pueblo. Occupied since about 1300, this Tewa pueblo was first described by Castaño de Sosa in 1591 as a square structure, two stories high with a central plaza.

The byway turns north on N.M. 520, traveling through Chimayó, a community known for its fine Spanish weaving and crafts, tasty food and famous church. The beautiful Santuario de Chimayó is especially known for El Posito, a hole in the floor of a side chapel filled with healing earth. Pilgrims come here to take a bit of the earth and pray for healing. The walls of an adjoining chapel are covered with religious paintings and statues, crosses, rosaries and crutches left by those who have sought healing. During the Easter season, the road to Chimayó is filled with people who have walked many miles on their various journeys. The village was founded in the early 18th century around a defensible plaza, and it still retains that pattern.

The byway next follows N.M. 76, climbing northeast through the creased and crinkled badlands, polka-dotted with scrubby piñon and juniper. Enormous mountains soar from the horizon. A slight detour takes you through Córdova, its dwellings sprawled along a narrow road that wends through a valley. The village is noted for its traditional wood carvers.

At Truchas, the byway makes a

Opposite: The village of Truchas was the setting for the film version of John Nichols' book, Milagro Beanfield War.

Photo by James Orr

Tribal members recently restored San Lorenzo de Picuris Church at Picuris Pueblo.

Photo by Mike Stauffer, N.M. Tourism Department

turn toward other destinations, but to truly appreciate its beauty, drive farther east into the village. The road through the village runs alongside a deep canyon. Buildings may seem to be precariously placed on its rim, but some of them have been there for generations. Looking east, you have the illusion of being on top of the world, but you're brought back to reality when you look west to Truchas Peaks, rising 5,600 feet above the village. This frontier outpost was built in a square with an entrance just wide enough for one cart to pass through, for defensive purposes.

Heading toward the village of Las Trampas, a wide expanse of valley opens out in panoramic beauty, with the barren Truchas Peaks punctuating the eastern horizon. More than 13,000 feet in elevation, Truchas Peaks are among the highest in the New Mexico Rockies. Settled in

1751, the village of Las Trampas has one of the finest surviving 18th-century churches in New Mexico, San José de Gracia, built in 1760 (generally open Friday and Saturday). All of the church's original paintings have survived.

Take a short one-half mile detour north at the junction of N.M. 76 and N.M. 75 to Picuris Pueblo. Its church, the third built at this pueblo, dates from the 1770s. It is unadorned adobe, except for small plants growing on top of the buttresses and a Pueblo ladder leaning against a wall. After visiting Picuris, turn back south on N.M. 75 through Peñasco to N.M. 518. Turning north here, a pullout (milepost 51.5) overlooks the pastoral beauty of Placita and the valley that shelters it. Farther down the road, a pullout on U.S. Hill (milepost 61.2) provides a view of the Carson National Forest in all its grandeur. The Taos Mountains dominate the view, with Wheeler Peak (at 13,161 feet, New Mexico's highest) towering over them all.

On down the road is the Carson National Forest's Pot Creek Cultural Site (milepost 66.4). The gate to the parking lot is locked to prevent pot hunting, however, you can park on the road and walk up. A one-mile loop trail leads to a kiva and a reproduction of a Pueblo room. Signs along the trail interpret the lifestyle of the prehistoric inhabitants of the area.

Cruise on through the villages of Talpa and Ranchos de Taos. An old Spanish *camposanto* (cemetery) brightens the view with flowers of every hue and crosses of every description among the traditional low marble gravestones.

What better way to end the trip than at the St. Francis Plaza in Ranchos de Taos.

St. Francis welcomes you, his bronze arms lifted toward heaven. The church named for him is the focal point of the Plaza. The San Francisco de Asis Church was made famous by the many artists and photographers who have tried to capture the essence of its massive adobe walls, glistening with straw. The interior is austere in its simplicity. Whitewashed walls contrast with dark-stained vigas and the Christmas colors of the *reredos* behind the altar. Instead of stained glass, two plain-glass windows illuminate it from either side.

The church shares the plaza with private homes and Andy's La Fiesta saloon. Recently renovated shops and galleries alternate with collapsing adobe structures. A purple coyote fence coexists with more traditional turquoise window frames. Red roofs, red *ristras, ranchero* music blaring from a boom box—these are some of the remembrances you will take home from the High Road to Taos.

—Laurie Evans Frantz

Below: The playful light on the thick adobe walls of the San Francisco de Asis church in Ranchos de Taos fascinates photographers.

Photo by Mike Stauffer, N.M. Tourism Department

Waves of Change

I often resist change. I ignore clues indicating it's needed and march forward, until life breaks apart and I'm forced to accept the new. But a recent trip to Peñasco, along the High Road to Taos Scenic Byway, helps me better understand life's transitions.

The town of some 275 residents has experienced waves of change over centuries, each bringing its own new vision. I start my exploration with the area's earliest inhabitants at Picuris Pueblo. Some 332 residents still live in many ways like their ancestors did, dating back to A.D. 1050, when their days and spirituality centered around nature and the seasons. I can see remnants of this ancient history in the Upper Plaza, where houses built from raw adobe stand above ceremonial kivas hidden underground.

The village church, a 1770s Mission-style treasure, stands as a reminder of the next wave of change that came to the valley. In 1591, the Spanish colonists arrived here, initiating a rich farming tradition that remains today. Headed back to Peñasco, I pass irrigated alfalfa fields and small home gardens. I also find galleries where traditional Hispanic artists carve *santos* (representations of saints sculpted in wood) and paint *retablos* (paintings on wood panels).

I make my way through town to Sahd's, the local general store, where I find in a big Quonset hut, pliers, nails and cans of Campbell's tomato soup. This store is run by a family from Lebanon that moved here in 1946, part of a post World War II phase, when many newcomers came to the state, including my family.

Yet another wave of change is notable farther down the street in an art gallery, where I find whimsical paintings, pottery and woodcarvings, remnants from the hippie days. During the 1960s many young people came to northern New Mexico to experience the solitude and simplicity of country life. Some set up in communes, while others settled in small towns like this.

Yet farther along, in a building covered with murals, I meet Peñasco's most recent wave, what I'll call the imaginative creators. These talented visionaries have come seeking a place to express themselves fully. Two chefs have moved here from San Francisco and opened a bistro. Next door at the 1940s Peñasco Theater, a performance company has moved in, presenting entertainment ranging from cabarets to puppet shows.

As I head back onto the High Road, the world seems more open and friendly, as I recognize the promise in its waves of change.

Colorful murals cover a building in Peñasco that houses a performance company and bistro.

Photo by Lesley S. King

Opposite, inset: A doorway at Chaco Culture National Historic Park reveals a dramatic landscape.

Photo by James Orr

TRAIL OF THE ANCIENTS . . .

1. Ship Rock Peak
2. Aztec Ruins National Monument
3. Salmon Ruins
4. Two Grey Hills
5. Casamero Pueblo
6. El Morro National Monument
7. Ice Cave and Bandera Volcano

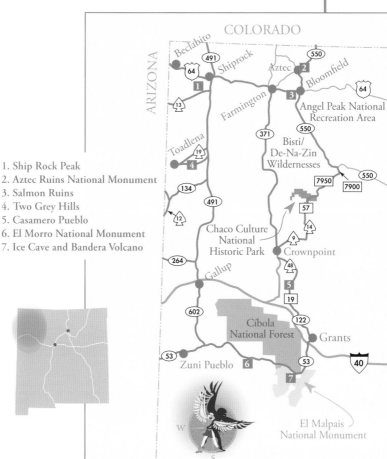

Who would expect a UNESCO World Heritage Site at the end of a rough road in the middle of a desert wilderness?

This is Chaco Canyon, the center of the Trail of the Ancients Scenic Byway. A remote area such as Chaco may seem like a strange place to begin your journey, but this byway isn't tidy—it has roads sticking out all over the place. Chaco is as good a place as any to start.

The best route to Chaco Culture National Historical Park is C.R. 7950 south from U.S. 550; the route is clearly marked and the dirt road safe for any vehicle (except during extremely rainy or snowy days). The 26-mile drive to the visitor center allows time to reflect on how this barren landscape could have supported a community as large as Chaco Canyon. A paved road near the center loops through the arid canyon, providing access to six monumental sites and trails leading to other sites.

Between A.D. 850 and 1250, Chaco Canyon functioned as a ceremonial center for the Ancestral Puebloan people; its influence was felt for hundreds of miles. Its remains still inspire awe. Undulating 2-foot-thick walls, constructed of small, thin tablets of sand-colored stone, loom in front of the massive canyon walls in an uneasy coexistence. Large slabs of canyon wall appear ready to fall onto the buildings. Indeed, this isn't an idle threat; it has happened before.

Driving south out of the park, you'll pass through some of the loneliest country you're likely to find anywhere. Once on N.M. 371, drive south to Crownpoint, well known for its monthly Navajo Rug Auction. South of Crownpoint, the byway

Opposite: Many Chaco outliers dot the landscape along the Trail of the Ancients Scenic Byway.

Photo by James Orr

Wildflowers bloom on Mount Taylor, near Grants. The mountain is sacred to many of the local tribes.

Photo by Steve Larese

leaves N.M. 371 to follow Navajo Road 48, which dead-ends at C.R. 19. Here the byway turns right and winds through sandstone buttes right out of a John Wayne Western. You'll arrive at Casamero Pueblo, a Chacoan outlier occupied circa A.D. 1050 to 1100.

Follow N.M. 122 to Grants, originally a coaling station for the Santa Fe Railroad. The discovery of uranium in the area in 1950 boosted the economy. The New Mexico Mining Museum re-creates a uranium mine. Grants is at the northern end of El Malpais (the badlands) National Monument; the byway passes through it on N.M. 53. El Malpais, created by lava flows as recent as 3,000 years ago, provides a variety of recreational opportunities. Prehistoric volcanic activity also

Traditional trading posts can still be found along the Trail of the Ancients Scenic Byway.

Photo by Steve Larese

formed the Ice Cave and Bandera Volcano, located about 25 miles southwest of Grants. The insulating properties of the surrounding lava and the ice cave's shape combine to maintain the freezing temperature in the cave. From Bandera, you can see more than a dozen cinder cones aligned in the Chain of Craters, a 20-mile stretch of cinder cones created by underground lava flow.

Driving west, El Morro (the headland) appears suddenly on the horizon like a huge ocean liner. Its waterhole made El Morro an important stop for travelers in the region, who often carved their names in the soft sandstone walls of the butte. Now a national monument, its history is written in stone for all to see.

N.M. 53 passes through Zuni Pueblo on its way to the Arizona border. The six original Zuni pueblos were the legendary Seven Cities of Gold sought by Francisco Vasquez de Coronado. The present pueblo was settled in 1699. Murals depicting Zuni's summer and winter religious observances in Our Lady of Guadalupe Mission provide a revealing glimpse into the pueblo's culture.

Heading north on N.M. 602, Gallup is the next destination. The city is famous for pawnshops that line its streets and sell Indian crafts. The visitor center hosts Indian dances from July to September. A mural on South Second Street honors the World War II Navajo Code Talkers. Classic movie fans should visit the El Rancho Hotel, where many actors stayed while filming near Gallup. Photos of them and their movies line the walls of the mezzanine. The Rex Museum presents information about Gallup's early coal-mining history.

The drive on U.S. 491 north out of Gallup leads to two trading posts famous in the history of Navajo weaving, Toadlena and Two Grey Hills. Toadlena is run like an old-time trading post: in return for rugs, it supplies cash, services and goods for about 1,500 Navajos living nearby.

The byway heads to Farmington on U.S. 64. The Navajo name for Farmington is Totah (the meeting place of waters). Two-thirds of the surface water in New Mexico flows through Farmington in the La Plata, Animas and San Juan rivers. Five miles of trails on the Animas River offer recreation for nature lovers and cyclists. The Farmington Museum provides information on the city's history, with exhibits about the oil and gas industry and a reproduction of a trading post.

With its wealth of water, it's not surprising that the Farmington area

Travelers throughout the ages stopped at El Morro. Many leave their names carved into the sandstone butte.

Photo by Steve Larese

A mano and metate *(tools for grinding corn) at Aztec Ruins National Monument remind us of the Ancestral Puebloans who once lived there.*

Photo by Steve Larese

was a busy place in prehistoric times. The ruins of two pueblos are open to the public: Aztec Ruins National Monument in nearby Aztec and Salmon Ruins near Bloomfield. Both of these Chacoan outliers were settled in the 11th century.

If you've always wanted to go to the moon but never had the opportunity, visit New Mexico's badlands. The Bisti Wilderness Area, the De-Na-Zin Wilderness and Angel Peak National Recreation Area can all be accessed from the byway. The erosion of geological strata of varying colors and resistance created the fantastically colored and shaped formations of the badlands.

The drive west on U.S. 64 to the Arizona border captures the essence of the Trail of the Ancients. The road descends a canyon filled

Colorful geological formations create spectacular vistas at the De-Na-Zin Wilderness.
Photo by James Orr

with yellow- and gray-striped hills. The bright green swath of an arroyo dazzles among subtle earth tones. Knobby red sandstone formations guard the Navajo community of Beclabito, where traditional hogans dot the landscape. Ship Rock rises at seven-o'clock. A sign at the border reminds you that you're in the Land of Enchantment.

—Laurie Evans Frantz

Journey to Another World

O ne day, in the second grade on the dusty playground of Alvarado Elementary School in Albuquerque, I bragged to my friend: "We went *past* the volcanoes."

I was referring to a weekend trip my family had taken to the Gallup Inter-Tribal Indian Ceremonial. Actually, many times I'd traveled much farther from home than the half-day drive, and I now know that my awe at the distance had more to do with culture than miles.

Even today when I attend the Ceremonial and watch a feather-bedecked dancer twirl and feel the drums beat in my heart, I'm amazed by the other-worldliness of "Indian Country" and the Trail of the Ancients Scenic Byway.

At the Crownpoint Rug Auction, I've run my palm over the silky strands of a masterpiece Navajo weaving and sat riveted as the auction price for it climbed to thousands of dollars, the gavel finally dropping, and the auctioneer yelling "sold!"

In both Gallup and Farmington, I've perused the trading posts to admire intricately tooled Zuni needlepoint jewelry, black-and-white striped Hopi *katsina* clowns and hand-shaped Acoma pottery.

Always finishing my expeditions hungry, I've relished the food native to the region: a Navajo taco—chile, cheese and onions over fry bread—or better yet, a mutton sandwich—mutton and a roasted green chile pepper folded into a tortilla.

But the most meaningful in all my travels has been meeting the denizens of this land and hearing the stories they tell. At the historic Toadlena Trading Post and Museum, which dates back to 1909, I met Clara Sherman, one of the master weavers of the region. When I encountered her, she had been weaving for some 80 years.

Clara took my hand and led me back to a spot in the store where

Clara Sherman, a Two Grey Hills master weaver,
stands in front of her creations.

her rugs hang—large ones with bold, intricate patterns, each design resonating poetically throughout the piece. She told me about learning to weave when she was 13.

"These are all from my head," she said, tapping her temple. In that brief sentence, she claimed a workmanship that is often copied, and a legacy that reflects the ancients who once traveled this trail.

LA FRONTERA DEL LLANO . . .

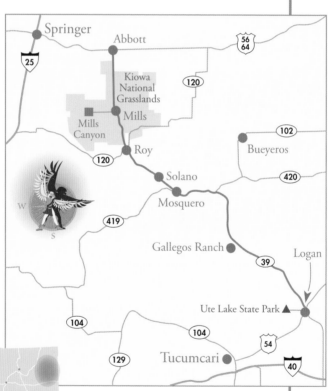

Springer
Abbott
56 64
25
Kiowa National Grasslands
120
Mills
Mills Canyon
102
120
Roy
Bueyeros
Solano
420
W
Mosquero
419
S
Gallegos Ranch
Logan
39
104
Ute Lake State Park ▲
104
54
129
Tucumcari
40

La Frontera del Llano Scenic Byway, the edge of the plains in Spanish, starts at Abbott, a place you'd think wouldn't warrant a name if there weren't a sign there to prove it.

Most of the byway (N.M. 39) runs through Harding County, where cattle outnumber people 7 to 1. The county has a population of about 650, less than one person per square mile.

It may seem strange that there is a national forest in Harding County, but it's true. The northern part of the byway runs through the Kiowa and Rita Blanca National Grasslands, a unit of the Cíbola National Forest. This is a forest of grass, the rolling short grass prairie of the southern Great Plains. This vast rangeland covers 99.7 percent of the county.

Driving south through the grasslands, you encounter the small community of Mills, named for Melvin W. Mills, lawyer, rancher, banker, territorial legislator and entrepreneur. A sign directs travelers west to the Mills Canyon Campground. The first six relatively flat miles are deceiving. After it leaves flat land, the road enters the Canadian River Canyon and becomes narrow, rocky and suitable only for vehicles with high clearance.

The campground is located at the site of the Orchard Ranch. In the 1880s, Mills planted 12 miles of land along the Canadian River with melons, tomatoes, grapes, cabbages and 14,000 fruit trees. He built the Mills Canyon Hotel, once a popular vacation spot that serviced a stagecoach line. The water that made the enterprise possible ended it in 1904, when the flooding Canadian River

Opposite, inset: Rain nourishes the grassy plains and brings rainbows to grace the open skies.

Photo by Steve Larese

wiped out orchards, irrigation system and buildings. All that can be seen now are the shells of a few stone buildings.

Roy, another 10 miles south on N.M. 39, is pretty quiet now, but it once thrived. The Dawson Railway was constructed through the area in 1906 to link Tucumcari to the coalfields in Dawson. During the 1920s and '30s, dry ice was produced here because the town overlies the Bravo Dome carbon dioxide field. Roy was a central shipping point for beans, wheat, cream and eggs until the Dust Bowl ended most farming in the 1930s. Roy's main streets are lined with buildings from an earlier era, like the red brick Floersheim Mercantile Company. Incorporated in 1897, it was one of the largest mercantile enterprises in northern New Mexico.

Music was a big part of the local social life. The late Roy Self played in a band with the town barber. The barber played the fiddle and was something of a composer, having written a popular tune that he called the "Spanish two-step." After two years as a full-time barber and part-time musician, James Robert Wills moved to Tulsa, shortened his name to Bob, and renamed his tune "San Antonio Rose." Wills' signature "ahh-ha" would bring Roy's one local policeman running to make the band keep the noise down.

Workers constructing the Dawson Railway settled Mosquero, 18 miles south of Roy and the Harding County seat, in 1906. The last cattle trail created by Charles Goodnight, marking the end of his operations in New Mexico, passed through this area. Today Mosquero is primarily a cattle ranching community.

The byway is adorned with a number of beautiful little mission churches. Like a string of pearls they

Opposite: The roadrunner, New Mexico's state bird, frequently races along the state's scenic byways.

Photo by Mike Stauffer, N.M. Tourism Department

stretch from Solano to Gallegos. Solano's Union Church was built in 1912 of native stone. The coat hooks made of horse shoes in the foyer remind you that you're in ranch country. Its folding wooden seats were taken from the school gymnasium in 1913. St. Joseph's Catholic Church in Mosquero was created from a school and the teacher's house in the 1930s, when a transept was built between the two buildings to join them.

South of Mosquero, the road descends David Hill in switchbacks. The plains, mottled with the shadows of clouds, stretch as far as the eye can see. At the bottom of the hill, N.M. 102 branches off to the east from the byway. The oldest and most beautiful of the mission churches, Sacred Heart of Jesus, is at Bueyeros (place of the oxen drivers), 18 miles from N.M. 39. The stone church has turquoise trim and a copper steeple. The wall behind the altar is painted like stained glass, in jewel tones of rose, turquoise, gold and pink. The altar rail, painted in the same colors, resembles a miniature Victorian fence. The confessional is from Santa Fe's Cathedral Basilica of St. Francis of Assisi, and the baptismal is 100 years old.

Back on N.M. 39, the Church of the Immaculate Conception at Gallegos Ranch was built in 1876 and replaced in 1914 with the present building of red sandstone.

Large Italian statues stand on its fine altars. All of these churches are kept locked, but neighbors have the keys.

The byway ends 94 miles from Abbott in Logan, best known for Ute Lake State Park on the Canadian River. Its recreational opportunities—camping, boating, picnicking and fishing—are inviting excuses to linger awhile.

—Laurie Evans Frantz

Opposite: Ute Lake, a Canadian River Reservoir, is one of the longest lakes in the state at nearly 13 miles.

Photo by Mike Stauffer, N.M. Tourism Department

Below: Retirees love the rewards of fishing at Ute Lake.

Photo courtesy of N.M. State Parks

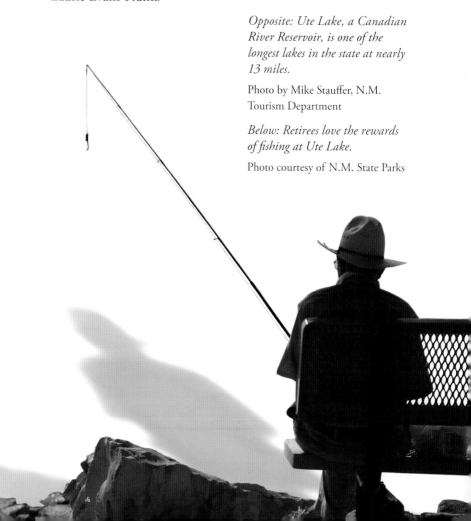

Plain Talk

I spent much of my life riding horseback on New Mexico's eastern plains, so today as I embark on La Frontera del Llano Scenic Byway, I feel right at home. Growing up out here I came to see that the way people talk reflects these wide-open spaces. Often ranchers will stand around a barn saying nothing at all, until a few words eke out, followed by a few others, and then minutes more of silence.

That's what this drive is like, miles of silence punctuated with moments of meaningful conversation. My friend Bob Bachen from Solano, a stop along the route, describes Harding County through which this byway passes:

The Big Empty
We offer you nothing.
No noise,
No pollution,
No traffic.
Harding County, no place like it.

Ranch kids learn about Dutch-oven cooking at an early age.

I reflect on this as I make my way to the first bit of conversation—the village of Roy. Though the town's main support—ranching—has dwindled in recent years, there is evidence of a new lifestyle. In shops along the main street, I find treasures made by locals: *santos* by Leroy L. Trujillo, CDs of cowboy poetry by Doc Mayer and lariat baskets and painted gourds by Rod and Gina Judy. While perusing one shop, I even run smack into Brad Pitt. After a brief swoon, I realize it's just a life-size cardboard cutout.

Only some 20 miles separate Roy from the next bit of conversation, Mosquero. On the town's main street, I encounter elaborate murals. Students at Mosquero Public Schools, along with area painter Doug Quarles, have illustrated the town's story both past and present on the general store, restaurant and bar. These include life-size depictions of the town's characters and area ranchers.

I head out of Mosquero back into the silence. As I gaze across hundreds of miles of open prairie, I acknowledge that this area really does live up to its name as The Big Empty. But along the side of the road a herd of antelope grazes, while a red-tailed hawk circles above. Clearly, as Bob's poem illustrates, the area is full of life's most profound communication.

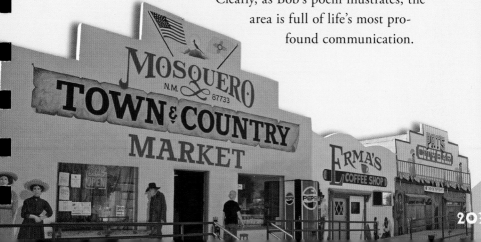

AUTHORS . . .

Laurie
Photo by Arnold Vigil

Lesley
Photo by Julien McRoberts

Marti
Photo by Scottie Dunshee

L aurie Evans Frantz is the Scenic Byways coordinator for the New Mexico Tourism Department and has directed that program for almost 10 years. Her degrees in anthropology and education, and her long tenure with the New Mexico Department of Transportation as an archaeologist and a transportation planner, have given her experience she feels makes this job a good fit for her. She is passionate about the Scenic Byways program and enjoys working with the state's community and business leaders, as well as other state and national agencies in promoting New Mexico's program.

L esley S. King, a native New Mexican, is author of *King of the Road,* a book of travel essays, along with many travel guidebooks, including *Frommer's New Mexico* and *New Mexico for Dummies.* Her articles have appeared in *The New York Times, Audubon Magazine* and United Airlines *Hemispheres* magazine, and she pens the monthly "King of the Road" column in *New Mexico Magazine.* King is also a photographer and she shot all of the images that accompany the "Roadside Attractions" essays in this book.

M arti Niman has lived and worked from Africa to Alaska as a salmon fisherman, gallery director, dog "musher," illustrator, audio producer, game warden, editor and park ranger. She now makes her home in Santa Fe and continues to explore New Mexico's spectacular backcountry with her Alaskan malamute, Oso. Niman says writing and photographing the Scenic Byways series was a welcome opportunity to explore and document parts previously unknown to her across New Mexico.

CREATE YOUR OWN SCENIC BYWAY MEMORIES . . .

Please use this handy checklist to help document your trips on
New Mexico's Scenic Byways.

Name of Byway	Date Traveled
J-9 Narrow Gauge Railway	
Wild Rivers Back Country	
Enchanted Circle	
Jémez Mountain Trail*	
Puye Cliffs	
Santa Fe National Forest	
Santa Fe Trail*	
Historic Route 66*	
Corrales Road	
Turquoise Trail*	
Mesalands	
Salt Missions Trail	

Name of Byway	Date Traveled
Abó Pass Trail	
Socorro Historical District	
Quebradas Back Country	
Trail of the Mountain Spirits*	
Geronimo Trail*	
Lake Valley Back Country	
Billy the Kid*	
Sunspot	
Guadalupe Back Country	
El Camino Real*	
High Road to Taos	
Trail of the Ancients	
La Frontera del Llano	

* National Scenic Byways